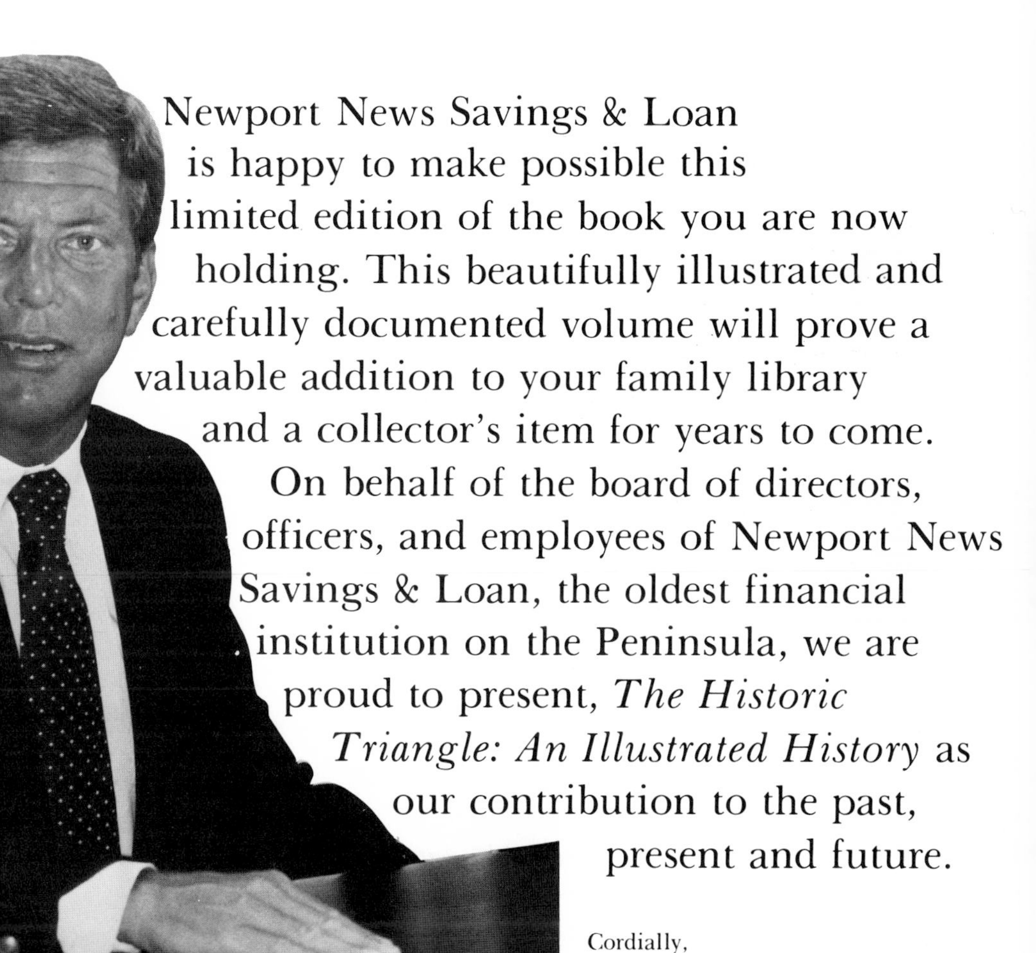

Newport News Savings & Loan is happy to make possible this limited edition of the book you are now holding. This beautifully illustrated and carefully documented volume will prove a valuable addition to your family library and a collector's item for years to come. On behalf of the board of directors, officers, and employees of Newport News Savings & Loan, the oldest financial institution on the Peninsula, we are proud to present, *The Historic Triangle: An Illustrated History* as our contribution to the past, present and future.

Cordially,

J W Hogge Jr.

President

AN ILLUSTRATED HISTORY

# The Historic Triangle

by Van Hawkins
with Bea Kopp

Designed by
Jamie Backus

Donning Company/Publishers
Virginia Beach, Virginia

*Prior to the reconstruction of Williamsburg's capitol, reopened in 1934, a monument noted the location of the original building, and these three youngsters posed atop the stone for a picture.*




For information, write: The Donning Company/Publishers, Inc., 5041 Admiral Wright Road, Virginia Beach, Virginia 23462.

Printed in the United States of America

Library of Congress Cataloging in Publication Data:

Hawkins, Van, 1946-
The historic triangle.
1. Jamestown, Va.—History—Pictorial works.
2. Jamestown, Va.—Description—Views.
3. Williamsburg, Va.—History—Pictorial works.
4. Williamsburg, Va.—Description—Views.
5. Yorktown, Va.—History—Pictorial works.
6. Yorktown, Va.—Description—Views I. Title

F234.J3H34 975.5'4251 79-11063
ISBN 0-915442-69-8

**For My Parents**
**Van and Bette Jo**
**Hawkins**

# Contents



*England was blessed in the 1600s with some extraordinary sea captains who enabled the British to defeat the Spanish Armada. In this reconstruction from Jamestown Festival Park, Queen Elizabeth thanks three captains for their explorations and naval victories: kneeling, Sir Martin Frobisher; center, Sir Francis Drake; right, Sir Henry Lee. Drake also led a British naval force which sailed around the globe.*

# Preface

Jamestown, Williamsburg, and Yorktown remind one of the phoenix, that legendary bird which rose from its own ashes.

As difficult as it is to believe, these towns, which played such critical roles in American history, for many years dwindled in size and importance, half-forgotten, until the twentieth century. But they live again because of the spiritual and financial resources of farsighted individuals who recognized that the past can teach us about the present and future.

The many facets of these historic towns offer a glittering array of subjects for a writer, but it is the purpose of this book to illustrate how the towns proved central to periods and events that led to the founding of this country.

This portrait in pictures and words presents the towns and their priceless treasures—the people, places, and principles that gave birth to and nurtured the United States of America.

To write about Jamestown, Williamsburg and Yorktown is to experience *deja vu*. Cornwallis, Pocahontas, Jefferson: they bring to mind words on pages read many years ago in a grade school history class in a small Missouri town. The knowledge then that one day the words would become less distant might have produced more attentiveness, but maybe not. Even so, studiousness then would not have greatly affected my apprehension now about writing of Virginia's historic triangle.

So many elements of the area have been written about, and so many knowledgeable people work and study in Tidewater, that tackling the subject had its unsettling moments. Fortunately, the scholars and people with expertise are as gracious as they are erudite. Many of them were kind enough to spend their valuable time helping find information that had eluded me or locating just the right illustration to enhance the pictorial history. Some even had the steadfastness to review the completed manuscript for accuracy and style of presentation.

I would like to thank Mike Schaffer, a historian and talented journalist, for taking time to read the book and offer some excellent suggestions. Francie Bailey, a historian with the National Park Service's Yorktown center, tolerated numerous visits and questions with grace and good humor; Francie helped me locate needed photographs from park service files, and she and park service historian Margaret Micholet read the completed manuscript and made numerous valuable recommendations. Pat LaLand, a Colonial Williamsburg Foundation representative, provided invaluable cooperation and access to Colonial Williamsburg materials and a careful review of my work to ensure accuracy. Pat also brought to the association a warmth and friendliness that made the project a pleasure. Many other persons and organizations allowed the use of their materials and provided help and encouragement. To them I am enormously grateful, and many are mentioned in the picture credit section of this book. I especially want to thank Bea Kopp, who took most of the contemporary photographs and reproduced many of the old ones. Bea is a good friend and an even better photographer. And as with almost everything I do, I must acknowledge a tremendous debt to my wife Ruth. I doubt that it could have been accomplished without her.

# Introduction

As it is in many dramas, profit was a major motivation in efforts to establish an English colony in America. And as the attempts at colonization unfolded, misfortune and failure plagued the players.

Sir Humphrey Gilbert was the first Englishman granted a charter to colonize the New World. Gilbert received the charter from Queen Elizabeth in 1578, but he died when his ship was lost at sea after an aborted attempt to plant a colony on the American continent. Gilbert was the half-brother of the English adventurer Sir Walter Raleigh, and they had more than blood in common. Raleigh also dreamed of colonizing the New World, and after he had acquired Gilbert's charter, he dispatched two shiploads of colonists on the long and arduous journey across the Atlantic Ocean.

The Englishmen landed on Roanoke Island off the coast of North Carolina, but little was accomplished by the expedition other than naming the territory Virginia in honor of England's "Virgin Queen" Elizabeth. Raleigh's second expedition sailed in 1585 under the command of Sir Richard Grenville. A fort was established on Roanoke Island, and an irony surfaced that would reappear throughout the first years of English attempts to settle in America: the Roanoke colonists starved despite the bounty of plants and animals in America. When Sir Francis Drake visited Roanoke Island during one of his raiding ventures against the Spanish, the remaining colonists returned with him to England.

The next attempt at colonization remains one of history's greatest mysteries. An expedition with about 150 settlers left England in May 1587. They, too, landed at Roanoke Island and embarked on the precarious existence that awaited Englishmen in the New World. The group included Eleanor Dare, who gave birth to Virginia Dare, the first English child born in America.

Unfortunately, war with Spain forced England's attention away from the struggling colony, and supply ships weren't sent until 1590. The supplies were unnecessary, however, because the settlers had disappeared. The relief ships found the fort abandoned and overgrown with weeds. The word "Croatan" was carved on a gatepost, and, according to Virginius Dabney (*Virginia: The New Dominion*), "seemed to indicate that the colonists had gone to Croatan Island, but no trace of them was ever found. . . . The Croatan Indians of Southeastern North Carolina, known today as Lumbees, believe that the blood of these lost colonists flows in their veins." Bad weather forced the relief ships back into the ocean, and the settlers—if they still lived—were claimed by a dark and foreboding continent—thus creating the mystery of the "Lost Colony."

Despite the failure of early efforts to colonize the continent, Old World interest did not slacken. If anything, the fever rose to a higher degree. There were exceptions, however. According to one account, Philip II of Spain offered as punishment to three thieves the choice of deportation to the New World or death, and one chose death.

The English were blinded by the glitter of

gold and other riches the Spanish had torn from the Indians in South America but there were other, less material, considerations, too. Politicians recognized the need to establish a foothold in America to counter Spain's growing empire. Religious leaders recognized an opportunity to spread Christianity among the savages. Adventurous men recognized the possibilities for searching out a quicker water passage from Europe to China. Mercantilists recognized the financial possibilities, so the London Company was formed in 1606. James I granted a royal charter, which stipulated that councillors in England and in Virginia would govern the colony, and a more organized attempt at colonization was under way.

One hundred and forty-four settlers and seamen were stuffed aboard the one-hundred-ton *Susan Constant,* commanded by Captain Christopher Newport; the forty-ton *Godspeed,* commanded by Captain Bartholomew Gosnold; and the twenty-ton *Discovery,* commanded by John Ratcliffe. Newport, an experienced privateer, commanded the fleet, which left London in December 1606, but bad weather held it near shore until February 1607.

After the long journey across the Atlantic, including stops in the Canary Islands for water, the tiny fleet arrived in the Caribbean Islands. The only fatality of the trip occurred as members of the expedition went ashore. One settler, Edward Brooke, died on one of the small islands, according to a fellow traveler, when the "fat melted within him by the great heat and drought of the country."

The apprehensive explorers left the Caribbean waters, and they sighted Virginia on April 26, 1607. After going ashore at Cape Henry, where they were not-so-warmly greeted by Indians who attacked them, the Englishmen opened a box containing names of the councillors authorized to govern the colony: Newport, Gosnold, Ratcliffe, Edward Maria Wingfield, George Kendall, and Captain John Smith.

The personal and political feuding characteristic of the colony's early days had already begun. Smith was confined when the colonists arrived, having been accused of taking part in a mutinous scheme. Twenty-seven years old when he arrived in the New World, Smith was an adventurer and mercenary. Although he initially was not allowed to sit on the council, Smith soon became a dominant force in the colony.

The explorers sailed into the Chesapeake Bay and spent several days searching along the James River for a spot to settle. On May 13, they found a flat, marshy peninsula almost three miles long, connected to the mainland by an isthmus. The location offered some valuable attributes: it was far from the coast and difficult for the Spanish to attack, it could be easily defended, and it was accessible to the ships, which could be tied to overhanging limbs of trees along the shore. But the location had drawbacks, unknown at the time, which would cost the colony hundreds of lives and untold misery before the enterprise was established on a firm footing.

*The Colonial Parkway near Jamestown*

# *Jamestown*

Englishmen set foot on what they named James Fort on May 14, 1607, and immediately began construction of a triangular, wooden stockade for protection. Before the fort was constructed, however, they were attacked by Indians controlled by the powerful Chief Powhatan. The Indians—who painted or tattooed their bodies, wore skins decorated with shells, and stuck bones and feathers in their hair—were members of one of the more than thirty tribes of Algonquins controlled by Powhatan. Although as lively and fascinating to look at as the Virginia countryside, their decorations belied a cunning that soon became apparent to the colonists. One man was killed and several were wounded in the first attack.

The colonists planted wheat and vegetables when they arrived and began domesticating the wilderness of their immediate surroundings. If Indian hostility seemed a clear and present danger, nature proved a more subtle and formidable foe. The location, which at first seemed so well-suited to their needs, became an enemy. The soil was poor, the water was impure, and disease-bearing mosquitoes swarmed about the low, marshy land.

To complicate their predicament, many of the settlers were more concerned with finding gold than with the hard work necessary for survival. The indolence of some made them their own worst enemies. Contrary to their expectations, the ground was not littered with gold. All they found was "fool's gold," and their foolish persistence in pursuing get-rich-quick ventures and their disregard for self-discipline almost proved their undoing.

A few miles downstream from Jamestown was an abundance of fish, crabs, and oysters, but there were periods when many of the adventurers starved to death. As fatigue, hunger, and sickness mounted, dissension swept the group. Fortunately, Smith gained control of the beleaguered colonists. His disciplinary measures brought a degree of industriousness from many of the indolent Englishmen, and a measure of stability was maintained.

Still, life at Jamestown was especially demanding

and crude. The vast forests provided materials for houses and furnishings such as benches and stools. Later, wattle-and-daub and frame houses were replaced with brick structures. The bricks were produced in the colonists' kilns. Artisans included carpenters, coopers, potters, brickmakers, and boat builders. Efforts at growing food the first few years failed to yield significant results, so colonists bartered with Indians and lived off the bounty of fish in Tidewater rivers and bays. Trade with the Indians included the exchange of beads, cloth, and pots for fish and game.

In December 1607 Smith earned a permanent niche in American folklore during an exploration of the Chickahominy River. America's archetypal adventurer was captured by Indians and later taken to Werowocomico, Powhatan's village on the York River, where the chief ordered that the Englishman's head be bashed in on a rock. According to Smith, he was saved by the chief's twelve-year-old- daughter Matoaka, who also was known by the name Pocahontas. After being saved from an unpleasant death, he returned to Jamestown, where squabbling continually plagued the colonists and a fire destroyed many of their supplies and wooden structures.

In the meantime, Newport had returned to England in command of the first of several voyages to transport additional colonists and supplies to Jamestown. His return in 1608 with settlers and supplies was particularly timely. He also brought two women, and one, Ann Burras, later married John Laydon in the first English marriage in the United States. Their daughter Virginia was the first child born in Jamestown.

Smith had been elected president of the colony, and he alone seemed capable of governing the bickering group that inhabited Jamestown. The population expanded when another supply fleet arrived in August 1609, bringing approximately four hundred settlers and a new company charter. Many of the colony's political problems had resulted from the governing authority being a council rather than an individual. To solve the problem, the London Company created a new charter that established a governor with substantial powers. Under the charter, Sir Thomas Gates was appointed interim governor, to be followed by Thomas West, Lord de La Warr. But a hurricane had separated Gates' ship, the *Sea Venture*, from the other ships of the fleet, and he did not arrive with them. Newport and John Rolfe were among the persons on the *Sea Venture*, which was stranded in Bermuda, and the incident provided material for William Shakespeare's play *The Tempest.*

*Sir Walter Raleigh, as much as any Englishman, was responsible for colonization of North America. This adventurer and soldier financed several attempts that ended in failure, but he did manage to name Virginia for the "Virgin Queen" Elizabeth. Raleigh's interests were diverse: in addition to being a soldier and explorer of some achievement, he aided Edmund Spenser in the poet's efforts to publish* The Faerie Queen. *Raleigh authored his* History of the World *while imprisoned in the Tower of London for treason. Although he escaped the executioner on that charge, he later was beheaded.*

Smith refused to relinquish leadership of the colony because Gates had not arrived to claim the governor's title. Under his demanding rule the tiny colony prospered until late in 1609, when he was seriously injured by the explosion of his gunpowder. The stocky, abrasive leader returned to England to recover from the wound, and he never saw the colony again.

Neither Gates nor Lord de La Warr had arrived in Virginia by the winter of 1609-10, and George Percy, one of the colonists, had to lead the settlers during their worst years—the "starving time." Starvation, disease, and Indians decimated the colony during the harsh winter. Only about sixty of 490 persons survived the period. Colonists were forced to consume their livestock, roots, and berries. When an Indian was killed, he was eaten by the desperate Englishmen. Some colonists supposedly dug up the bodies of other colonists and made meals of the corpses.

*The Englishmen who sailed to the New World found existence more harsh and dangerous than they had imagined. The Indians, however, were at home in the wilderness. Despite some hostility, they frequently helped the colonists survive by trading food for goods. This Indian lodge at Jamestown Festival Park provides an accurate view of an Indian dwelling at the time of the founding of the colony.*

*The English colonists who landed at Jamestown found the area occupied by Indians of the Powhatan Confederacy, which consisted of almost nine thousand Indians from about thirty different tribes. The confederacy was controlled by Chief Wahunsonacock, who called himself Powhatan after his favorite village. Powhatan's attitude toward the Englishmen fluctuated until his daughter Pocahontas married John Rolfe in 1614, and a brief friendship ensued. In this engraving at left from Captain John Smith's* General History of Virginia, New England, and the Summer Isles, *Powhatan and other Indians are depicted in one of the encounters Smith claimed to have had with them.*

*The Virginia colonists owed a considerable debt to Captain Christopher Newport, depicted in this Allan Jones, Jr., mural, unveiled in 1957. Newport was selected to organize and transport his countrymen to Virginia. He brought them safely to the New World and helped keep them alive through several trips to England for supplies and additional colonists. He is shown here landing after his initial voyage at what is now Newport News.*

*Full-scale reconstructions of the* Susan Constant, Godspeed, *and* Discovery *rest at anchor at Jamestown Festival Park. The vessels, recreated for the 350th anniversary of Jamestown, offer a glimpse of how crowded life must have been for the adventurers who set sail in the winter of 1606. The London Company chartered the three ships, all of them old. The* Susan Constant *and the* Godspeed *had been used in the coal trade to northern European ports. Very little is known of the original ships except their tonnage. Griffith Baily Coale, the artist who created the painting of their arrival which hangs in the Virginia State Capitol in Richmond, painstakingly researched ships of the period. Robert G.C. Fee, in a paper presented to the Society of Naval Architects and Marine Engineers in 1958, recounted his lengthy research and calculations in creating first a scale model of the* Susan Constant, *and later as naval architect for the project, the contract plans for each ship. According to Fee, the* Susan Constant *and the* Godspeed *made seven round trips from England to Jamestown and may ultimately have returned to service as colliers. The* Discovery *remained in Virginia waters after her 1607 arrival. It was from this vessel that the area of Cape Cod was charted in 1609, and these charts may have assisted the* Mayflower *on her arrival in 1620. The fate of the* Discovery *is*

The situation was bleak, to put it mildly, when Gates finally arrived in May 1610. Men aboard the *Sea Venture* had constructed two boats to transport them from Bermuda. The dilemma of the colonists was so dire that Gates decided the best course was to board their ships and return to England. By an amazing coincidence, as the colonists were sailing down the James River to abandon the colony, they met a long boat dispatched by Lord de La Warr, who was anchored at Mulberry Island with supplies, and the colony was saved.

Somewhat surprisingly, a few Englishmen continued to come to Virginia, which had proved to be a financial burden, rather than a boon, to investors. The ship that brought Ann Burras to the colony also brought supplies and men to establish a glassmaking industry. The glasshouse was located about a mile from Jamestown, now known as Glasshouse Point. But the business, undertaken by eight Germans and Poles, failed.

Although timber and several other raw materials were shipped to England on a limited scale, the colony was never a going concern until John Rolfe's experimentation with tobacco. Rolfe's efforts produced a quality tobacco that proved commercially viable. Ironically, tobacco brought an economy that saved the colony, but it launched the South on an agricultural course that led eventually to the Civil War. Rolfe's first acceptable shipment of what James I called the "stinking weed" left Virginia in June 1613. While developing a commercial crop for the colony, which would grow to shipments of about one-half million pounds in fifteen years, Rolfe provided physical security as well. His marrige to Pocahontas in Jamestown Church in 1614 helped produce an era of good feeling between Indians and Englishmen that lasted until the bloodbath of 1622. Tobacco became the staple crop in Virginia, and it produced two side effects of significance: cultivation of the crop quickly depleted the soil's minerals, and growing tobacco brought a great need for labor.

Charles E. Hatch's booklet in the E.G. Swem-edited series of *Jamestown 350th Anniversary Historical Booklets* describes Jamestown in 1614 as consisting of "two faire rows of howses, all of framed timber, two stories, and an upper garret or corne loft high, besides three large and substantiall storehouses joined together in length some hundred and twenty foot, and in breath forty....In the island [were] some very pleasant and beutifull howses, two blockhowses...and certain other framed howses."

The first wattle-and-daub houses in Jamestown were replaced by brick structures as the 1600s progressed.

*A major attraction at Jamestown Festival Park is the reconstructed James Fort, a full-scale replica of the triangular palisade built by the settlers in 1607 for protection against Indians and Spaniards. Soldiers and settlers in costumes staff the fort and help exhibit the eighteen wattle-and-daub structures that provided primitive protection for Jamestown's early inhabitants. A reproduction of the first church constructed in Jamestown, in the center of the palisade, is the largest structure in the fort. Built in part in 1607, the early church was expanded later as the fort population grew.*

*The reconstructed wattle-and-daub structures in James Fort at Jamestown Festival Park are as primitive inside as outside. The land about the village provided colonists with both food and furnishings; fruit and game from the countryside became their food, and the vast forest provided trees for houses and furnishings. Despite the abundance of game, settlers relied heavily on the grain bartered from Indians, and even then, hundreds starved during the colony's early history.*

Under the governorship of Sir Thomas Dale, colonists were granted private plots of land, which ended the collectivism of the first years. The colonists' industriousness increased appreciably, illustrating the failure of America's first experiment with a crude form of communism. The agricultural economy and colony gained momentum as trade with England increased. During 1619 more than one thousand people arrived in the colony, many of them Englishmen who came as indentured servants, working for several years to repay persons who had paid their fares.

The first blacks who arrived in the colony in 1619 were indentured servants. A Dutch ship visiting the colony traded twenty blacks into servitude for supplies. As blacks continued to arrive in Virginia, a solution to the colony's labor problems appeared. As surely as tobacco claimed the riches of Virginia's soil, it claimed the freedom of black men and women. To ensure availability of labor to maintain the tobacco economy, Virginia's General Assembly established laws to bind blacks to a lifetime of slavery.

*Many of the crafts that helped Englishmen survive and flourish in Virginia's historic triangle have been preserved by contemporary artisans. A young woman in colonial dress displays the art of candlemaking at Jamestown Festival Park. Re-creating the colonial technique involves dipping wicks of woven cord into pots of melted tallow and beeswax. The result—the principal source of artificial light for hundreds of years.*

*The London Company's original effort to colonize Jamestown was a male-only effort. The 104 adventurers, including gentlemen from prominent families and others with not-so-high connections, had one thing in common—a need to band together in order to survive. They began building a fort immediately upon deciding the location of their settlement on the peninsula; protection from the Indians required constant vigilance. Robb Storm, left, and Lee Hubert reenact the roles of early settlers as part of Jamestown Festival Park's re-creation of the historic settlement.*

*In addition to providing stern and resourceful leadership that enabled the struggling colonists at Jamestown to survive the rigorous challenges of Virginia's wilderness, Captain John Smith provided useful information about North America through his explorations and recordings of his findings. This seventeenth century woodcut of Smith is from his* General History of Virginia, New England, and the Summer Isles, *published in 1614. The 1612 map of Virginia reflects Smith's view of the area, the result of his many explorations.*

In an effort to entice more people to settle in Virginia, the Virginia assembly was established by a new charter in 1618 sent out by the London Company. The new charter called for a legislative assembly in the colony, introducing a self-governing process that would become an integral part of American life. The charter created a House of Burgesses (elected representatives) and continued the Governor's Council (representatives of the king). The first General Assembly was convened by Governor George Yeardley at Jamestown Church in July 1619, and twenty-seven members attended. The London Company's progressiveness would later prove harmful to British interests, however, for once given the right of self-rule, Virginians would fight to retain it.

As tobacco reduced and exhausted the soil, and as planters continually drew upon new land to produce their crops, plantations began to spread throughout Tidewater

*Contemporary craftsmen re-create the art of glassmaking in the glasshouse at Jamestown. The colonists tried glassmaking in 1608, when the London Company sent European glassmakers to aid the English. The always fragile enterprise broke after the production of a few bottles, glasses, and windowpanes. The glassmakers used river boulders to build their furnaces. Ingredients included potash from wood fires, sand from the river shore, soda imported from England, and lime, possibly slaked from local oyster shells. These contemporary workers make their glass articles in much the same manner as the early craftsmen. The present-day glasshouse is situated at Colonial National Historical Park beside the original location.*

This fence winding its way along a Virginia peninsula field recalls the state's agricultural heritage—a heritage begun by the colonists who arrived at Jamestown. After their feverish search for gold produced only "fool's gold," many of them realized that the soil was itself rich, so they became farmers. Efforts to produce such things as flax for linen and mulberry trees for silk ended in failure, but with John Rolfe's successful experiments with tobacco, the colony's economic potential was ignited.

This map of the Jamestown area from 1607 to 1619 indicates how little of Tidewater Virginia was settled during the period. For protection, Englishmen remained close to the settlement during the early years. When the urge for expansion sent them beyond the borders of the small settlement, most of them still remained near the James River.

Virginia. By the 1620s Tidewater had almost thirty plantations. Early plantations usually were owned by several men, each of whom had a share in the profits. This spreading out made Indian attacks all the more effective, since settlers found themselves in isolated, vulnerable positions. The ascendancy of Opechancanough as head of the Powhatan Confederacy brought organization to the hostilities. The culmination of the wily chief's plotting occurred on the morning of March 22, 1622. At a prearranged time, Indians struck colonists up and down the James River. No one was spared in the "Good Friday Massacre." Approximately 350 out of about 1,250 settlers were killed, including Rolfe. About one-fourth of the colony's population and property was destroyed in the surprise attack.

*This Sidney King painting re-creates a portentous episode in American history: a Dutch ship visiting Jamestown in 1619 traded twenty blacks into servitude for supplies. Although blacks at first were indentured servants, like many whites who worked to pay for their passage, Virginia law was later changed to allow blacks from Africa to be held perpetually as slaves.*

*Although there have been many important legislative events in Virginia and United States history, perhaps the most important was the first meeting of the General Assembly. In July 1619 Governor George Yeardley convened the assembly of twenty-seven members at Jamestown. It was the beginning of self-rule in this country, and colonists found the right worth fighting for. This painting by Elmo Jones portrays the historic meeting in Jamestown Church.*

*In this 1974 photograph, taken at Colonial National Historical Park at Jamestown, Allen Hardy reenacts the life-style of early settlers. The colonial militiaman-farmer tilled his tobacco crop with one eye on his armor and weapons in case of Indian attack. The production of tobacco provided colonists a salable product which became an economic staff of life to the English. John Rolfe's first tobacco crop in 1612 grew to 2,500 pounds produced in the colony by 1616. Rolfe somehow obtained seed of the sweet-scented Trinidad tobacco, unlike the harsh, biting Indian tobacco, and thus began a multi-million-dollar business in the United States.*

Jamestown was saved by Chanco, an Indian boy who was living on the plantation of his godfather, Richard Pace, an Englishman. Rather than murder his benefactor, as Chanco had been ordered to do, he warned him of the attack. Pace, in turn, rowed across the James River and alarmed the settlement, and the inhabitants were armed and ready when the Indians attacked. The colonists put up a stout defense with polearms, swords, muskets, pistols, and cannons, and, confronted by sturdy resistance, the Indians withdrew.

The Indian attack was followed by additional troubles—plagues in 1622 and 1625. But Jamestown expanded, and by 1624 there were 183 people in the town. New Towne, the area outside the Jamestown fort, had developed by the time James I dissolved the London Company in 1624 and Virginia became a royal colony. The settlement consisted of a church, guardhouse, a few stores, and more than thirty houses.

When the losses of the London Company led James I to disband the company, and with it the General Assembly, colonists displayed an independent spirit that would later erupt, much to the discomfort of Great Britain. Members of the dissolved General Assembly met in May

1625 to devise a way of convincing James I to continue the assembly and to protest the lack of wisdom in trade measures he had imposed. The assembly next met in March 1628, after the death of James I and the succession of Charles I.

By the time Sir William Berkeley became governor in 1642, there were more than fifteen thousand people in Virginia. The period brought another Indian massacre when Opechancanough led a surprise attack in 1644, and about five hundred colonists were killed. Retaliation was merciless until the Indians signed a treaty in 1646 and were driven westward.

Berkeley was a popular and productive governor until Charles I was overthrown and beheaded in January 1649 during the Great Rebellion in England. Berkeley denounced Parliament's action and remained loyal to the monarchy. The governor stepped down only when a fleet sent by Oliver Cromwell arrived. The loyalist Berkeley returned as governor of the colony when Charles II ascended to the throne and Britain's monarchy was restored.

One of the colony's worst years came during Berkeley's second term as governor. In 1667 the colony's tobacco crop was devastated by a hail storm and a hurricane. The

*This painting by Sidney King conjecturally depicts the first tobacco crop at Jamestown. John Rolfe's first successful crop was planted in 1612 and supposedly was located both inside and outside the palisade. Pocahontas, who married Rolfe in 1614, sits in the foreground. At the rear a ship can be seen in the James River, moored by the pier at Jamestown. Rolfe, born in 1585 at Heacham in the Shire of Norfolk, England, sailed with his first wife for Virginia aboard the* Sea Venture, *but the journey ended badly when the vessel was wrecked in Bermuda in 1609. A daughter was born to the couple in Bermuda, but the child died before they sailed again for the colony. Rolfe's first wife died soon after their arrival at Jamestown in May 1610.*

This Sidney King painting depicts Green Spring Plantation, home of Governor William Berkeley, near Jamestown; it is adapted from Benjamin Latrobe's painting of the old house as it appeared about 1796. At far left is the drying house, and at right is the greenhouse for cultivation of tobacco seedlings.

The horror of the 1622 Indian attack is conveyed in this Theodore de Bry engraving. Algonquin tribesmen surprised the colonists, and the "Good Friday Massacre" brought death to almost 350 of the English settlers. Although about one-third of the population was annihilated, Jamestown was saved because Chanco, an Indian youth, warned the Englishman with whom he was living. The Englishman in turn warned Jamestown in time to avoid catastrophe.

*In this illustration by Howard Pyle, the cavalier appearance and demeanor of Governor William Berkeley, right, is apparent. Berkeley, who became governor in 1642, was at first a popular leader. When he again became governor in 1660, he was criticized and then attacked by a group of frontier Virginians led by young Nathaniel Bacon, Jr. "Bacon's Rebellion" began with a disagreement as to how marauding Indians should be dealt with, but the controversy eventually spread to other political issues as well.*

Dutch, who were at war with Great Britain, contributed, too. Six Dutch ships sailed into Hampton Roads and destroyed several merchant vessels loaded with the colonists' tobacco. .

Berkeley had been greatly admired during his first governorship. He was a gifted man and effective leader, but the older Berkeley who became governor again in 1660 seemed to be a different individual. He was head of a powerful and wealthy faction in the colony. When the governor acted too slowly in dealing with marauding Indians who threatened settlers on the western edge of the colony, an opposing faction of Virginians, led by young Nathaniel Bacon, Jr., took matters into its own hands. Bacon was leader of a group of rebellious colonists who sought a more vigorous and firm policy for dealing with the Indians. Headquartered at Middle Plantation—later Williamsburg—Bacon and his followers attacked the Indians without the governor's approval. Through a show of arms, they also forced several egalitarian measures from

*In this drawing Nathaniel Bacon, Jr., reads to some of his followers. The young leader of many Virginia colonists posed a serious threat to the rule of Governor William Berkeley, and fighting between the factions broke out in 1676. But Bacon died of an illness, and without their leader, the followers were unable to carry on an effective fight against the aristocratic Berkeley and his supporters. "Bacon's Rebellion" came to an end, and so did the lives of many of Bacon's men.*

*Although Jamestown Island was later fortified with Confederate coastal guns during the Civil War to prevent Union ships from going upriver to Richmond, the island was largely neglected after 1776. This 1854 painting by R.M. Sully of Jamestown portrays its appearance at that time.*

*The 250th anniversary of the founding of Jamestown was celebrated in 1857 with an encampment on the island. The excitement of soldiers and a parade brought a swarm of men, women, and children to view the spectacle as boats glided under sail along the James River. The next time soldiers visited the island was for a more serious purpose—construction of earthworks during the Civil War. The celebration is captured in an illustration from* Harper's Weekly *of June 27, 1857.*

the House of Burgesses.

Despite a lull in hostilities between the two factions, animosity smoldered. In one of American history's many ironies, violence erupted in 1676—exactly a century before the American Revolution—as rebellious colonists took up arms against royal authority. In September Berkeley's forces were routed at Jamestown, and Bacon's men burned the settlement, which consisted of the statehouse, church, some frame houses, and about a dozen brick homes. The governor and his followers took refuge on Virginia's Eastern Shore.

Death interceded in the struggle against Berkeley when Bacon died in October 1676, and without their charismatic young leader, the rebels were subdued by the governor's forces. The rebellion was almost completely crushed by the time Colonel Herbert Jeffreys, the king's investigator, arrived from England with commissioners and troops.

After Berkeley regained control, he took revenge. When one thousand British troops arrived from England, the governor was executing captured leaders of the revolt. He displayed a lack of mercy that didn't endear him to the already-dissatisfied Virginians. Berkeley hanged more

*In 1907 a woman takes a moment to study the James River from the boat landing at Jamestown pier before joining other passengers for a Sunday school picnic. The pier was not always so deserted, as illustrated by another 1907 photograph showing the pier crowded with people. In the background are the church, at center, and, at right, the first stages of the Jamestown Monument.*

than twenty of the rebels, which purportedly prompted Charles II to remark, "That old fool has hanged more men in that naked country than I did for the murder of my father."

There had been fitful sentiment for a college in Virginia, and in 1690 a committee was appointed to plan for the institution. Through the efforts of Lieutenant Governor Francis Nicholson and the Scottish minister James Blair, who was the Bishop of London's commissary and who presented a petition to the king and queen requesting a charter, permission was obtained in 1693 for establishment of a college by King William and Queen Mary. The Reverend Blair, also rector of Jamestown Church and a powerful man, as many governors learned to their sorrow when they clashed with him, was named first president of the College of William and Mary. The college was to be located at Middle Plantation, which had been patented by Doctor John Pott in 1632, and the foundation for the first building was laid in 1695.

Jamestown's statehouses had been the scenes of many heated debates concerning royal authority. But when the fourth statehouse burned in 1698, Virginia's burgesses decided to move the capital to Middle Plantation, which was named Williamsburg in 1700 in honor of King

*The new Jamestown Visitor Center, completed appropriately in 1976, exhibits many artifacts unearthed in excavations at Jamestown. The center's museum includes parts of guns, swords, and breastplates and domestic items such as earthenware, tools, and candlesticks. The center also offers a fifteen-minute film entitled "Jamestown." The center and the historic island are under the care of the National Park Service.*

*A 1931 aerial view of Jamestown shows the seawall that was constructed in 1900-01 to protect the historic island from erosion by the James River. Most of the original settlement—marked by the trees to the left of the monument—is gone. The Jamestown Monument and statues of Captain John Smith and Pocahontas are visible, as well as the tower of Jamestown Church, center.*

William. Jamestown went steadily downhill after the capital was moved in 1699. Vines and grass took over the island where Englishmen earlier had fought so hard to defend themselves. By the 1750s, the Jamestown area was a plantation site, owned primarily by the Travis and Ambler families.

A military post was located on the island during the American Revolution, and American and British prisoners were exchanged there. Confederate fortifications were constructed during the Civil War, but there was little further attention paid to Jamestown until preservation was undertaken in the twentieth century.

In 1893 Jamestown Island was owned by Mr. and Mrs. E. E. Barney. Much of the island had been worn away by the river, and many of the original brick foundations were claimed by the water. But a seawall was constructed in 1900 to protect the area from further erosion. The Barneys gave about twenty-three of the island's 1,500 acres to the Association for the Preservation of Virginia Antiquities in 1893, and the association, chartered in 1889, is largely responsible for saving what remains of Jamestown and for opening the site for public viewing. The remaining acreage was acquired later by the National Park Service as part of the Colonial National Historical Park.

The historic island was designated Jamestown National Historic Site in 1940, and since then, the National Park Service and the antiquities association have jointly maintained the island, including the historic church, excavated foundations that illustrate the size and location of the colony's houses, the reconstructed 1608 glasshouse, and a National Park Service information center. The center, constructed in 1976, features a film about Jamestown's history and a display of items found during excavations of

*The forcefulness and strength of spirit of Captain John Smith are conveyed by a statue honoring him. The bronze likeness was created by the late William Couper in 1907 and presented to the Association for the Preservation of Virginia Antiquities in 1908 by Mr. and Mrs. Joseph Bryan. Smith's early exploits as a mercenary earned him a coat of arms bearing three Turks' heads. The Englishman reportedly was granted the coat of arms by the Prince of Transylvania after defeating three Turks, who unwisely challenged him to combat. After his European adventures, Smith traveled to Virginia. In addition to providing leadership that enabled the constantly feuding colonists to survive, the short, stocky adventurer explored the region during several excursions. Burned when a bag of gunpowder exploded, Smith returned to England in 1609 to recover. After additional adventures, including crossing the Atlantic again for exploration, Smith concentrated on writing. He died in 1631.*

the island.

To celebrate the 350th anniversary of the settlement, Jamestown Festival Park was created in 1957. The park has an Old World Pavilion which illustrates events that led to the English settlement and a New World Pavilion that depicts Virginia's contributions to the development of the United States. The park also has full-size replicas of the *Susan Constant, Godspeed,* and *Discovery,* an Indian lodge, and a reconstruction of James Fort built in 1607 by the settlers. Administered by the Jamestown-Yorktown Foundation, a state agency, the festival park is located about one mile from the tiny island where America was born.■

*On a hiking trip to Jamestown Island in 1917, two young men named Carneal, left, and Brayshaw posed near the Pocahontas monument. Students at the College of William and Mary were among the more enthusiastic visitors.*

*This bronze statue of Pocahontas on Jamestown Island, sculpted by William Ordway Partridge, welcomes visitors with open arms. Pocahontas was only about twelve when she reportedly laid her head upon Captain John Smith's to save him from the death sentenced by her father, Chief Powhatan. Although Pocahontas allegedly saved Smith's life, she was fated to become intertwined with another famous Englishman, John Rolfe. After marrying Rolfe and in 1616 traveling to England with her husband and son Thomas, Pocahontas, or Lady Rebecca as she was then called, became ill and died during the visit. She was buried at St. George's Church at Gravesend, England.*

*Attractions at Jamestown Island include foundations illustrating the size and shape of many of the original buildings constructed by the colonists. Each site includes a painting of the original structure that closely reflects the appearance of the building, and historical background accompanying each painting provides perspective for the viewer. The original foundations and other ruins are marked above ground with brick and wood.*

*Religious services in Jamestown were first led by the Reverend Robert Hunt, who was the first Anglican minister in the New World. The Reverend Hunt read the Anglican service every day and twice on Sundays. A crude pulpit—a board nailed between two trees—soon gave way to a timber church constructed inside the palisaded fort. The colony's first brick church, the tower of which survives today, was begun in 1639 at the site of an earlier frame church erected outside the fort in 1617. To celebrate Jamestown's three hundredth anniversary, in 1907 a reconstructed church was placed adjacent to the old tower. That tower, with its arched entrance, stands just inside the fence. The addition extends behind it. Tourists today occupy its benches.*

*An interesting—if not altogether reliable—legend explains why this tree has grown between two graves in the graveyard at Jamestown's church. Buried in the graves are the Reverend James Blair and his wife, Sarah Harrison. The Reverend Blair, the first president of the College of William and Mary and a powerful figure in the colony, married Sarah Harrison when she was little more than seventeen and he was thirty-eight. The mother of the bride was unhappy with the marriage. Mrs. Blair died before her husband; when he was later buried beside her (he lived to be eighty), this tree grew between them and pushed the graves apart. The "mother-in-law" tree died and has been removed from the gravesite since the picture was made. A sapling remains.*

*No historical site would be complete without its own historical monument. In Jamestown, the Tercentenary Monument was erected in 1907 by the federal government.*

*Jamestown Festival Park opened on April 1, 1957, on the 350th anniversary of the first permanent English settlement in America. The twenty-acre park today includes pavilions with scenes that take visitors from the Old World to highlights of Virginia's history. The park is located one mile from Jamestown Island and is owned by the Commonwealth of Virginia.*

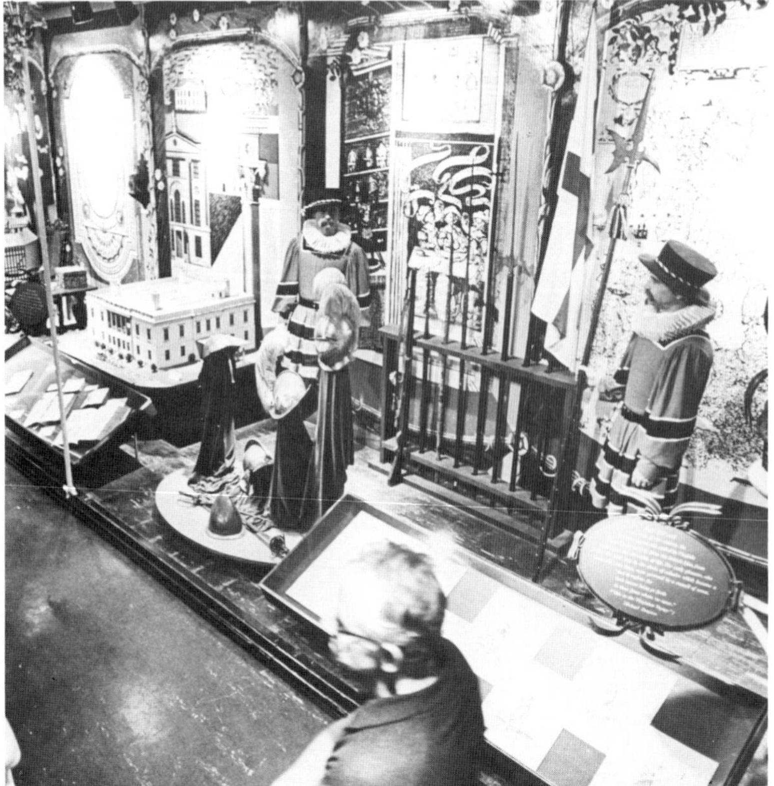

*Crime and punishment in the Virginia colony could be a grisly affair. Criminals received harsh and, by today's standards, often inhumane punishment. Minor crimes often meant the stock, for public payment of the debt owed to society. For these youngsters, however, the stock at Jamestown Festival Park means an enjoyable, not agonizing, experience.*

*This twentieth-century view of Jamestown Island indicates how much the island has changed since Englishmen came ashore in the 1600s. The first landing site has been lost to the James River, and the location of the original fort has disappeared. The town was originally three-quarters of a mile long. Twenty-five acres of the western end of the island also have been claimed by the river.*

*The Colonial Parkway near Williamsburg*

# Williamsburg

Williamsburg was as central to the founding of the United States as Jamestown was to the founding of Virginia.

Middle Plantation was settled in 1632 to protect colonists from hostile Indians and remained an insignificant settlement until it was chosen as the site for the College of William and Mary, which began taking shape in the late 1690s. Designed in the style of Sir Christopher Wren, noted English architect, the college's first building, the Wren Building, was begun in 1695. It was the first of the college's three original buildings. The others were the President's House and Brafferton Hall. The College of William and Mary's first commencement was held in 1700. Although the school received a severe blow in 1705 when the main building burned and the school's books were destroyed, Williamsburg and the college were on their way to prominence in colonial Virginia.

Middle Plantation consisted only of the remains of a palisade, the college, Bruton Parish Church, and a few houses when Virginia Governor Francis Nicholson began to lay out a new capital there in 1699. Nicholson originally planned the town in the shape of the capitals **W** and **M**, but common sense prevailed. Duke of Gloucester Street, a widened horsepath, was the town's main artery, and two parallel streets were named Francis and Nicholson by the governor, who was not burdened with excessive modesty. To provide spaciousness, plans called for Duke of Gloucester Street to be 99 feet wide and broad areas to be left for vistas and greens.

Under Nicholson's direction, the town began to take shape. The Capitol Building was begun in 1701, at the opposite end of Duke of Gloucester from the Wren Building, and the burgesses first met there in 1704, impatiently, a year before its final completion. The gaol was completed in 1704; the powder magazine and the present Bruton Parish Church in 1715 (the existing church was deemed too small); and the Governor's Palace in 1720, with remodeling and the addition of the ballroom wing in 1751.

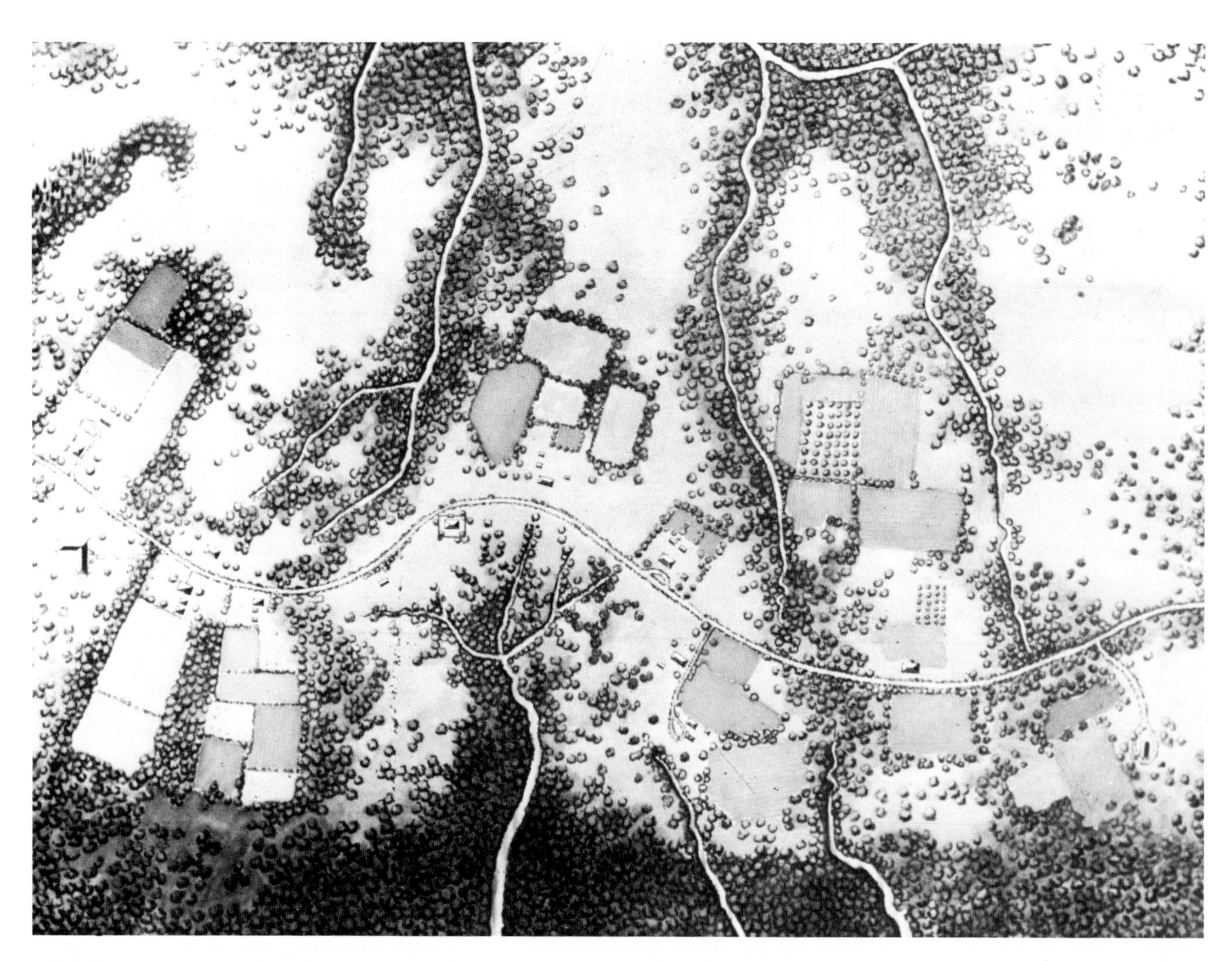

*This painting illustrates the fields and houses of Middle Plantation in 1699. The plantation was settled in 1632 to protect colonists from hostile Indians, but when it was chosen as the site of the College of William and Mary in the 1690s, it was destined to become a major center of activity in Virginia. Virginia's burgesses decided to move the capital from Jamestown to Williamsburg in 1699, and the town remained the capital of Virginia until the state government moved to Richmond in 1780.*

Although Nicholson laid out Williamsburg's first streets, Governor Alexander Spotswood, who took office in 1710, designed many of the buildings. As the public buildings were completed, so too were houses, taverns, and sundry shops. The town eventually contained nearly two thousand residents, except during Publick Times—periods when the General Assembly met in the spring and fall. During Publick Times Williamsburg swelled to between four thousand and five thousand people. Planters came from their great Georgian-style plantation homes throughout Tidewater, and cavaliers rubbed elbows with coonskin-clad frontiersmen in the dusty streets.

Plans for the town specified that each lot would be one-half acre, which gave the town an appealing spaciousness. The capital also possessed a beauty, grace, and charm that could not be overshadowed by the giant men who trod her streets to and from meetings that eventually would turn the world—the British world, at least—upside down.

Although Williamsburg had many craftsmen, most

*This engraving by R. de Hooge depicts King William and Queen Mary, who, in addition to approving funds to create the College of William and Mary, proved beneficial to their subjects in England as well. After their accession to the British throne, greater religious toleration was allowed in an attempt to end divisive religious issues. Parliament passed a toleration act to enforce the movement.*

*An engraving in* Williamsburg in Virginia *by Rutherfoord Goodwin depicts "a likeness of his majesty, King William III, in whose honor the City of Williamsburg in Virginia was named." William of Orange, king of England, Scotland, and Ireland, married his cousin Mary in 1677. They became rulers of England in 1689, and through a charter and funds granted by the royal couple, the College of William and Mary was founded in 1693, the second oldest college in the United States; only Harvard predates it.*

*One of the most influential men in colonial Virginia, the Reverend James Blair arrived in the colony as a missionary in 1685, but he soon became the Bishop of London's commissary. The Reverend Blair's marriage to Sarah Harrison, daughter of the influential Benjamin Harrison, increased his power in the colony, and he served as the first president of the College of William and Mary after obtaining a charter for the school from King William and Queen Mary in 1693. The portrait by Charles Bridges hangs in the Great Hall of the Wren Building.*

of the goods, particularly the grander items, were imported from England in exchange for tobacco. That exchange—raw goods for finished products—made the colonies valuable to England, which depended on markets for her manufactured products. The relationship was symbiotic, and Williamsburg closely reflected English tastes. Fashions, houses, entertainment—most were borrowed from England. Sometimes they were modified to suit the more primitive conditions in the colony, but they remained traceable to England.

The people of Williamsburg, which was incorporated as a city in 1722, were a lively lot; a noticeable *joie de vivre* existed in somewhat sharp contrast to their more

*Named for the noted English architect Sir Christopher Wren, the Wren Building at the College of William and Mary is still used by the college. Part of the original structure survived fires and modifications, and the building was restored between 1928 and 1931. Portions of the building are open to visitors, who can tread through rooms where Thomas Jefferson studied. The building also houses classrooms in use today as well as faculty offices. This series of photographs shows the exterior of the building, the Great Hall, an early classroom exhibit, and the view through a Wren Building window. The Reverend Hugo Jones, who taught at the college early in the eighteenth century, wrote that the building was "first modeled by Sir Christopher Wren and adapted to the nature of the country." Although this is not certain, it has been called the Wren Building since its restoration.*

*Fencing off the college campus has occupied more than one generation at the College of William and Mary. An 1880s view from the Wren Building, right, shows pickets being installed facing Duke of Gloucester street.*

*A somewhat later view, above, shows men digging fence posts on another side of the campus.*

stern, northern neighbors. And Williamsburg symbolized Virginia. Colonial Virginians loved entertainment, whether it was dancing the stately minuet or lively jigs accompanied by musicians or being entertained at the theater. In the 1730s, William Levingston built a theater, and a second theater was added in 1752, when Lewis Hallam's company arrived from England and premiered with Shakespeare's *The Merchant of Venice.* There was a racetrack near the town, and horse racing was quite popular, drawing viewers such as George Washington. Another popular amusement must certainly have been strolling in Williamsburg's lovely gardens.

Williamsburg was the hub of the expanding colony through most of the eighteenth century, and it also served as the conduit for communication through the newspaper *The Virginia Gazette,* which was established in 1736 by William Parks. J. A. Osborne's *Williamsburg in Colonial*

*One of the three original structures at the College of William and Mary, the Brafferton Building has fared well over the years and remains largely intact. Built in 1723, the building was constructed with profits from Brafferton Manor in England and was created for the education of Indian youths. Today the Brafferton Building is used for offices and has rooms for guests of the college.*

*A very early photograph of the three original buildings at the College of William and Mary shows the Brafferton Building, left; the Wren Building, center, and the President's House, right.*

*Lord Botetourt's statue stood on the campus of the College of William and Mary in this early photograph of the President's House at bottom left. The added porch and kitchen wing were to disappear in the restoration of the lovely building, and the statue was later moved for its own protection. Years of exposure to the elements and to the students who frequently painted the figure during various campus celebrations, had taken their toll. He now stands, splendid and secure, in the college library.*

*The President's House is the oldest college president's house in the country. First occupied in 1732, its famous guests have included Thomas Jefferson, Benjamin Franklin, Woodrow Wilson, and Queen Elizabeth II. Between 1928 and 1932 John D. Rockefeller, Jr., gave funds to restore the residence, which houses the college's presidents in eighteenth-century ambiance.*

The most majestic of Williamsburg's residences, the Governor's Palace served seven royal governors to the American colony. Originated by an act in 1699, the building was begun in the early 1700s and completed about 1720. It also was the residence of Virginia's first two governors after independence, Patrick Henry and Thomas Jefferson. Construction of the mansion began in 1706 and was supervised by Henry Cary, who made the drawings for the building. The present palace was carefully reconstructed on the original foundations and contains many fine antiques of the period.

*Times* provides an example of the liveliness with which the newspaper conveyed its information with an obituary published in January 1739:

Beneath this marble stone there lies
  Poor Tom, more merry much than wise;
Who only liv'd for two great ends,
  To spread his cash and love his friends.
His darling wife, of him bereft,
  Is only griev'd—there's nothing left.

Williamsburg, capital of the colony from 1699 to 1780, encompassed about three hundred houses in one square mile. Planters and visitors strolled by the shops, gazing through windows at the latest fashions and visiting with friends. During Publick Times, a circus-like atmosphere prevailed. Fairs and slave auctions were punctuated by the sounds of horses, children, and craftsmen hawking their wares on the town green.

Some colonial visitors to Williamsburg would gain prominence during the Revolutionary War. Many of the illustrious Virginians came for sessions of the House of Burgesses, which was something of an exclusive club of planters. Among its members were Peyton Randolph, who presided over the burgesses, George Washington,

*Inventories survive listing the furnishings of the palace in its early days. When reconstruction began, careful research resulted in the accurate appearance of its many rooms. This room boasts a gentleman's shaving stand.*

*The palace ballroom, which once was witness to stately dances, now echoes more often to the sound of tourists' feet. An opulent room, it is sometimes brought to life with the magic of music, played on antique instruments, in concert there.*

*Crystal and candlelight are part of the elegance of the palace dining room. In colonial days food was brought in covered containers. An invitation to dine with the royal governor was a mark of distinction.*

John Robinson, George Wythe, Edmund Pendleton, Carter Braxton, Richard Henry Lee, and Patrick Henry.

The inevitable break between Virginia burgesses and royal authority became noticeable when the Stamp Act became law in March 1765, despite Virginians' protests that it constituted taxation without representation.

The separation became an insurmountable schism between Virginians and British authority when John Murray, the Earl of Dunmore and governor of the colony, ordered gunpowder removed from the town magazine and stored aboard a British ship on April 20, 1775. Dunmore's decision was the result of a meeting of delegates held in March in Richmond at St. John's Church, where Patrick Henry introduced a bill to establish a Virginia militia, closing his argument with the familiar, stirring words, "I know not what course others may take, but as for me, give me liberty or give me death!"

Dunmore's decision brought Virginians, led by Henry, into Williamsburg, demanding return of the gunpowder or compensation, and the governor fled the city on June 8 with his family to take refuge on a British ship.

The fever of freedom burned as furiously as Wil-

*The palace gardens are extremely formal, with hedges and walks forming precise patterns. There is a maze based on the one at Hampton Court in London. This lovely greenery extends behind the main building of the palace.*

liamsburg's bonfires in succeeding months. Virginia patriot George Mason's Declaration of Rights was accepted by the General Assembly, and its principles later resurfaced in Philadelphia when the Declaration of Independence, written by College of William and Mary-educated Thomas Jefferson, was accepted by the colonies' representatives.

The Commonwealth of Virginia was established in June 1776, when representatives met in Williamsburg. Henry was elected governor, and a General Assembly of

*This centerpiece of restored colonial Williamsburg stands at one end of the Palace Green. Erected on the original foundations, the architecture reflects the grandeur of the crown, and the term "palace" reflects the temper of the colonists.*

*Dunmore's Cave, according to popular legend, was an escape route from the palace. Children believed the tale, and it became a somewhat dangerous playground as they searched for a nonexistent tunnel. It is the site now of a mound and ice house at the restored Governor's Palace.*

*The Governor's Palace, which was destroyed by fire in 1781, later became the site of the Matthew Whaley School, a full eleven-year school. The school, in turn, had to give way for reconstruction of the palace, which is due for refurbishing in early 1981.*

*In this 1942 photograph the palace garden gets a new tree.*

*In a 1933 photograph of the soon-to-be-demolished Matthew Whaley School, it is situated at the head of the Palace Green, and at left are some of the outbuildings that were restored on the grounds of the palace.*

elected delegates met in Williamsburg to run the affairs of Virginia without deference to the royal governor or British crown.

As the new nation was gaining strength, Williamsburg was declining. "An Act for the Removal of the Seat of Government" was passed in 1779, when Jefferson was governor. The capital was moved in 1780 to Richmond because that city was more secure from British attacks. Additionally, the colony had spread tremendously as pioneers pushed westward, so a central location was more suited to Virginia's governmental needs.

But some glorious days remained for Williamsburg. Washington stayed in the Wythe House when he arrived in Virginia for the siege of Yorktown in 1781, and plans for the siege were devised as Washington met with Comte de Rochambeau, commander of French forces. When the siege began, wounded Americans were housed in the Governor's Palace, and wounded Frenchmen were hospitalized in the Wren Building, as nearby cannons tolled the death knell of British power in the American colonies.

*The Virginia Gazette* and many of the town's businessmen left when the capital was moved to Richmond. Enrollment at the college declined, and in the late 1700s, the town's population was less than 1,500. Williamsburg's only major attractions were the college and a lunatic asylum, built in 1773 after the House of Burgesses passed provisions in 1769 for maintenance of the mentally

*Tracing its antecedents back to 1633, Bruton Parish, an Episcopal church, sits in the middle of the restored area in Williamsburg. The church at Middle Plantation proved too small when the plantation became Williamsburg and capital of the colony, so a new church was constructed between 1710 and 1715. Many of colonial Virginia's most gifted citizens worshipped at Bruton Parish Church, including George Washington, Thomas Jefferson, and Patrick Henry. The church survived the succeeding years well and is the scene of regular worship today. The large chair inside the church was reserved for the governor of the colony. The stone christening font (where Pocahontas may have been baptized) is thought to have been brought from the church at Jamestown.*

*Chowning's Tavern on Duke of Gloucester Street in Williamsburg still draws crowds of hungry visitors searching for a good meal and a refreshing drink. The original tavern was begun by Josiah Chowning in the 1760s and served ordinary people, unlike some of its competitors that catered to more elite patrons. The reconstructed Chowning's Tavern serves traditional lunch and dinner specialties such as Brunswick stew and Welsh rarebit.*

The King's Arms Tavern on Duke of Gloucester Street fed many of Virginia's most prominent citizens, including George Washington. The tavern, operated by Jane Vobe during the 1700s, is represented by this carefully reconstructed restaurant operated by The Colonial Williamsburg Foundation.

ill. The original building, the first public mental institution in America, burned in 1885.

The cannons that sounded the end of British influence may have signaled the end of Williamsburg's influence, too. In addition to the throngs of people, the city's charm and vivacity departed with the great orators who made the capital ring with words that would resound for centuries. As disinterest and decay robbed the town of its grandeur, fires struck its buildings. The Capitol Building, the Wren Building, Raleigh Tavern—all were gradually consumed by flames.

Although the town's galaxy of great men was gone, an occasional luminary still attached himself to the colonial capital. John Tyler, who became president of the United States in 1841, lived in Williamsburg from 1837 to 1842. But by the 1800s, the town had little more than twenty general stores, saloons, and restaurants.

The sleepy town found itself in harm's way in 1862, as General George B. McClellan brought Union troops up the peninsula toward Richmond, and Confederate forces, commanded by General Joseph E. Johnston, wait-

*Pewter mugs line the shelves of the barroom in one of the Williamsburg taverns, ready to provide ale and cider to weary visitors or townspeople concerned with refreshment after a day's work. Pewter, used extensively during the 1700s for kitchen utensils and plates for everyday use, was usually simple in design and remained popular until the 1800s, when glass came into fashion.*

*A sign that would lure any thirsty traveler and the greeting of a lovely hostess make Wetherburn's Tavern in Williamsburg an appealing sight. One of Williamsburg's open exhibitions, the restored tavern was completed in the late 1960s, but part of the historic building survived from the 1700s. The original proprietor, Henry Wetherburn, was a noted host of eighteenth-century Virginia, and the sumptuousness of his kitchen, which The Colonial Williamsburg Foundation has furnished with period utensils, explains his success.*

*The Ludwell-Paradise House was the first purchase by the Reverend William Archer Rutherfoord Goodwin when John D. Rockefeller, Jr., in 1926 decided to finance a restored colonial Williamsburg. With Rockefeller's backing, the Reverend Goodwin gradually acquired property that became the nucleus of the historic restoration. The Ludwell-Paradise House, which required only minor work to be restored to its colonial appearance, was constructed in the early 1700s and remained in the Ludwell family. Lucy Ludwell, while living in England, married John Paradise, and after his death she returned to Williamsburg in 1805 to live in the house until she was committed to the mental institution located in the town.*

ed at Fort Magruder east of Williamsburg. The outnumbered Confederates were forced to retreat after battle, and Union forces occupied Williamsburg for the remainder of the war.

The College of William and Mary, which was closed during the Civil War, reopened after the conflict. But the South was the scene of great suffering after the Civil War, and merely existing was enough challenge, much less supporting a college. So the college closed its doors in 1881 and didn't reopen until 1888, when the state awarded money to the College of William and Mary for education of teachers. Under the leadership of Lyon Tyler, son of President Tyler, the college began a long, arduous comeback.

During World War I, Williamsburg swelled to about fifteen thousand persons because it was surrounded by military bases. It became tawdry in nature, as historic old buildings were destroyed to make room for gas stations and other commercial enterprises. An explosives factory was built near the town in 1916, and it added to the boom.

Little remained of the town's colonial grandeur by the 1920s, except the college, several houses, and the insane asylum. In *Cows on the Campus*, historian Parke

*One of the most famous early inns was Christiana Campbell's Tavern on Waller Street. Mrs. Campbell relocated from what is now known as the James Anderson house to this building in the early 1770s. She served a substantial clientele until the capital was moved to Richmond and the town declined. The Colonial Williamsburg Foundation has reconstructed the tavern, which is now a restaurant.*

Rouse, Jr., quotes one person who summed up Williamsburg's existence: "Five hundred lazy live off five hundred crazy." Williamsburg's lethargy was best illustrated in 1913 by the city council's refusal to vote funds to have the clock in the Bruton Parish Church tower wound each week.

Time would not stand still for long. William Archer Rutherfoord Goodwin came to Bruton Parish Church as rector in 1902. Although he left in 1909, Goodwin returned to Williamsburg in 1923 as the College of William and Mary's director of endowment and professor of biblical literature and religious education. Goodwin had the vision to recognize the treasures that awaited in a restored colonial capital. In 1926 he recommended such a restoration to John D. Rockefeller, Jr., and a correspondence began that culminated in a visit by Rockefeller in November of that year. Rockefeller attended the dedication of the College of William and Mary's Phi Beta Kappa Hall; then he and Goodwin toured the town. Several days later, Goodwin received a telegram that read in part, "Authorize purchase of antique referred to in your. . . letter." The message was signed "David's Father," and Goodwin wasted no time in purchasing the

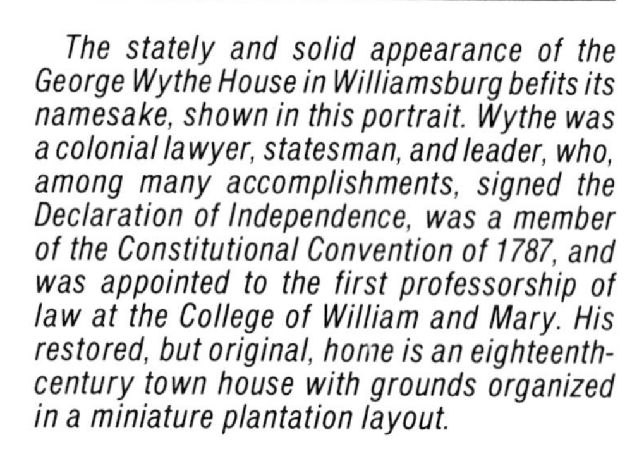

*The stately and solid appearance of the George Wythe House in Williamsburg befits its namesake, shown in this portrait. Wythe was a colonial lawyer, statesman, and leader, who, among many accomplishments, signed the Declaration of Independence, was a member of the Constitutional Convention of 1787, and was appointed to the first professorship of law at the College of William and Mary. His restored, but original, home is an eighteenth-century town house with grounds organized in a miniature plantation layout.*

"antique," the Ludwell-Paradise House on Duke of Gloucester Street. With Rockefeller as the anonymous financial backer, Goodwin began negotiating for properties that would become the backbone of the restored area.

Reconstruction of colonial Williamsburg, which did not begin from scratch because eighty-eight of the town's original buildings had survived, gained momentum as Perry, Shaw and Hepburn, a Boston, Massachusetts, architectural firm, was hired for the restoration. Work began with the Wren Building in 1928; then came the Capitol Building and Governor's Palace. By World War II about twenty million dollars had been spent on the undertaking. The war halted restoration, as attention to the past was overshadowd by concern for the present. When hostilities ended, work again got under way.

From its beginning, at which time Rockefeller anticipated spending "three or four, or even five millions of dollars" for property, restoration, and rebuilding, restored Williamsburg has grown to a remarkable mirror of

MAY 10, 1776. THE NUMBER 67.

# VIRGINIA GAZETTE.

ALWAYS FOR LIBERTY, AND THE PUBLICK GOOD.

ALEXANDER PURDIE, PRINTER.

PURSUANT to powers received from the Hon. the Continental Congreſs, the Committee of Safety are ready to grant commiſſions for making repriſals upon the property of the people of *Great Britain*, at ſea, or in the rivers, below high-water mark, to any perſons who ſhall apply for them, and comply with the terms mentioned by Congreſs.

EDMUND PENDLETON, preſident.

THE Committee of Safety deſire the commanding-officers of the ſeveral minute battalions to procure and return, without delay, an exact liſt of the number of men in each company, and how they are furniſhed with arms, that the ſame may be laid before the Convention.

EDMUND PENDLETON, preſident.

IN CONGRESS, *April* 11, 1776.

RESOLVED, that it be recommended to the ſeveral Aſſemblies, Conventions, and Committees or Councils of Safety, of the United Colonies, to uſe their beſt endeavours in communicating to foreign nations the reſolutions of Congreſs relative to trade.

*April* 16. Whereas much inconvenience may be derived to the publick from committees (other than the Committees of Safety in each colony) on the publick poſt roads, ſtopping and opening the mails, and detaining letters from the Conſtitutional Poſt: It is therefore reſolved, that no committees, but the Council or Committee of Safety in each colony, or ſuch perſon as they ſhall on extraordinary occaſions authoriſe, ſhould ſtop the Conſtitutional Poſt, open the mail, or detain any letters therefrom.

*Extracts from the minutes.*

CHARLES THOMSON, ſecretary.

IN the proteſt of the Lords againſt the prohibitory bill are the following paragraphs reſpecting the commiſſioners to be ſent to America, viz.

7thly. Becauſe the whole ſcheme of this predatory war of private lucre is put under the arbitrary direction of certain commiſſioners, to us unknown, even by name; who have power to give ſuch continuance to the ravages authoriſed by this bill as their arbitrary will ſhall ſuggeſt; to pardon, or except from pardon, any number or deſcription of perſons, and with poſes in view, has taken eſpecial care to provide as ſtrong a temptation as human nature, ſet above law and reſtraint, and furniſhed with every facility to corruption, can poſſibly be expoſed to.

8thly. Becauſe we know nothing of the buſineſs of theſe commiſſioners, farther than the above arbitrary diſcretion with regard to pardons. Rumour gives out, that they are to have a power to treat with the Americans for a redreſs of their grievances. Of this, however, neither the ſpeech from the throne, nor the bill, have given the leaſt intimation; although, if the commiſſioners treat on this ſubject at all, acts and powers of parliament being the matter of complaint, the commiſſioners ought to derive ſome previous authority from parliament, in order to give weight and efficacy to their negotiations, and to preſerve ſome appearance of dignity in ourſelves. It is hardly proper that parliament ſhould appear in no other light than as the inſtrument of penal reſtrictions, attainder, penalties, and confiſcations, as the maker of menacing addreſſes, and the rejecter of dutiful petitions. It is hardly decent to ſhow ourſelves fierce and inflexible here, but to be ſatisfied with permitting unknown perſons, whom miniſters ſhall chooſe in future to appoint, to diſpoſe in America of powers and acts of parliament at their pleaſure; leaving us firſt the odium of rejecting reaſonable requeſts, and afterwards the diſgrace of ratifying ſhameful conceſſions.

*The FORRESTER's farewel to CATO, &c. &c.*

TO THE PEOPLE.

IT is not a time to trifle. Men who know they deſerve nothing from their country, and whoſe hope is on the arm that hath ſought to enſlave ye, may hold out to you, as Cato hath done, the falſe light of reconciliation. There is no ſuch thing. 'Tis gone! 'Tis paſt! The grave hath parted us; and death, in the perſons of the ſlain, hath cut the thread of life between Britain and America.

Conqueſt, and not reconciliation, is the plan of Britain. But, admitting even the laſt hope of the Tories to happen, which is, that our enemies, after a long ſucceſſion of loſſes, wearied and diſabled, ſhould deſpairingly throw down their arms and propoſe a re-union; in that caſe, what is

Be not deceived. It is not a little that is at ſtake. Reconciliation will not now go down, even if it were offered. 'Tis a dangerous queſtion, for the eyes of all men begin to open. There is now no ſecret in the matter; there ought to be none. It is a caſe that concerns every man, and every man ought to lay it to heart. He that *is* here, and he that was *born* here, are alike concerned. It is needleſs too to ſplit the buſineſs into a thouſand parts, and perplex it with endleſs and fruitleſs inveſtigations, in the manner that a writer ſigned a *Common Man* hath done. This unparallelled contention of nations is not to be ſettled like a ſchoolboy's taſk of pounds, ſhillings, pence, and fractions. *That writer*, though he may mean well, is ſtrangely below the mark; for the firſt and great queſtion, and that which involves every other in it, and from which every other will flow, is *happineſs*. Can this continent be happy under the government of Great Britain, or not? Secondly, can ſhe be happy under a government of our own? To live beneath the authority of thoſe whom we cannot love is miſery, ſlavery, or what name you pleaſe. In that caſe, there will never be peace. Security will be a thing unknown; becauſe, a treacherous friend in power is the moſt dangerous of enemies. The anſwer to the ſecond queſtion, can America be happy under a government of her own, is ſhort and ſimple, viz. as happy as ſhe pleaſes; ſhe hath a blank ſheet to write upon. Put it not off too long.*

Painful as the taſk of ſpeaking truth muſt ſometimes be, yet I cannot avoid giving the following hint, becauſe much, nay almoſt every thing, depends upon it; and that is, *a thorough knowledge of the perſons whom we truſt*. It is the duty of the publick, at this time, to ſcrutiniſe cloſely into the conduct of their Committee Members, Members of Aſſembly, and Delegates in Congreſs; to know *what* they do, and their motives for ſo doing. Without knowing this, we ſhall never know whom to confide in; but ſhall conſtantly miſtake friends for enemies, and enemies for friends, till, in the confuſion of perſons, we ſacrifice the cauſe. I am led to this reflexion by the following circumſtance, that the gentleman to whom the unwiſe and arbitrary inſtructions to

*There was a lot of important news in 1776, and* The Virginia Gazette *reported it to Americans anxious to learn about events concerning their struggle for independence from Great Britain. The first edition of the newspaper was published on August 6, 1736, by William Parks. After* The Virginia Gazette *moved to Richmond in 1779, other weeklies were launched from time to time in Williamsburg, but with little success. Parks, who was a prominent citizen of Williamsburg, also started a paper mill near the town. He died in 1750 while on a trip to England. After Parks' death, William Hunter bought his printing establishment and became publisher of the* Gazette. *When he died in 1762, the paper was continued by Joseph Royal, and then by John Dixon and then Alexander Purdie. Somewhat confusingly, for a short time before the revolution, there were three weeklies all bearing the same name in Williamsburg.*

colonial times. The Rockefeller family has contributed about sixty-seven million dollars since 1926. Today The Colonial Williamsburg Foundation is a self-supporting educational foundation whose operating expenses are derived mainly from ticket sales; hotel and restaurant receipts; sales of reproductions, books, and records, and gifts and grants.

The restoration of colonial Williamsburg brought an invasion of visitors, but others marched, too, surrounding the historic area. Businessmen and professionals arrived, like their counterparts centuries earlier, in search of a home and financial opportunities. With a local economy largely dependent on tourists, businesses moved into the area to provide services for the sightseers. The "new" Williamsburg—motels, restaurants, shopping centers, public schools, assorted shops, and private residences—has created a sense of a town within a town. Williamsburg

*Committing the crime meant doing the time, even in colonial days. Virginians who stepped outside the law were held in the public gaol on Nicholson Street until the general court determined how they would pay for their trespasses. Both debtors and serious offenders were held in the gaol until 1772, when a change in the law largely eliminated the confinement of debtors. Punishment for law-breakers could be as minor as a fine or as major as death by hanging. Several of the pirate Blackbeard's band were held at the gaol in Williamsburg until they were tried and hung. The contemporary structure is restored and serves as an exhibition building for The Colonial Williamsburg Foundation.*

*One of colonial Virginia's most effective orators and leaders was Patrick Henry. A member of the House of Burgesses, the lawyer frequently traveled to Williamsburg for sessions held at the Capitol Building; there he made one of his famous speeches, criticizing the Stamp Act in 1765: "Caesar had his Brutus, Charles the First his Cromwell, and George the Third—may profit by their example. If this be treason, make the most of it." Henry's popularity led to his becoming the first governor when the Commonwealth of Virginia was created in 1776.*

*Although their resistance to English authority held dangerous consequences, the thirteen colonies were blessed with brilliant and determined leaders. When the unrest resulted in the Declaration of Independence, which was written largely by Thomas Jefferson, Virginia provided more than its share of leaders to sign the document. The seven Virginia signers are brought to life at the New World Pavilion in Jamestown Festival Park. They are, left to right, Francis Lightfoot Lee, Thomas Nelson, Jr., George Wythe, Benjamin Harrison, Carter Braxton, Thomas Jefferson, and Richard Henry Lee.*

now has 3,300 acres and 10,500 residents, but the town's energy is still generated by the college and historic area.

The Colonial Williamsburg Foundation continues its exhaustive research on the place and period as it proceeds to refine and enlarge the experience of returning to colonial times. By 1976 Williamsburg's eighty-eight, eighteenth-century structures had been restored, and the historic area consisted of approximately 130 acres. More than one million visitors a year experience historic Williamsburg, with its guides dressed in colonial clothes, its craft shops with artisans at work, and its buildings restored with painstaking attention to detail.

*The Capitol Building, reconstructed on the foundation of the original structure, is still used occasionally by the General Assembly of Virginia (every four years) to meet in commemorative sessions. The original Capitol Building was completed in 1705. It burned in 1747, and a second structure was built and used until 1779, when Richmond became the capital of the commonwealth. George Mason's Declaration of Rights, a precursor of the Delcaration of Independence, was adopted by burgesses in the Williamsburg Capitol. Inside the building are the conference room (with the long table), the hall of the House of Burgesses (with seats along the wall), and the chamber of the general court.*

Bringing it all back must at times have seemed like working a jigsaw puzzle with many of the pieces missing. That it succeeded illuminates the thread of inventiveness and determination that binds modern Americans to their ancestors who sailed across the Atlantic Ocean. ■

*A contemporary militiaman stands guard at Williamsburg's Public Magazine, which contains a collection of flintlock muskets and other arms. The more than 250-year-old magazine was the focus of conflict in April 1775, when a company of British marines confiscated about 750 pounds of gunpowder. The soldiers were 'under orders from the British governor, who had decided to disarm the colonists. The Americans were moving ever closer to an open break with British authority, but the confrontation over the governor's move was resolved when the colony's receiver-general paid for the powder.*

*The Powder Magazine is unique in that it was the forerunner to the restoration that was to come later under the auspices of John D. Rockefeller, Jr. By the 1880s the hexagon-shaped building, originally designed by Governor Alexander Spotswood, was serving as a stable. Part of a wall had been knocked out so horses could come and go.*

*A Baptist church of Greek temple design dwarfed the Powder Magazine when Williamsburg had lost its colonial elegance. This anachronism disappeared with the restoration.*

*A Hessian drum captured at the Battle of Trenton, when George Washington crossed the Delaware, is displayed on the top shelf, at left.*

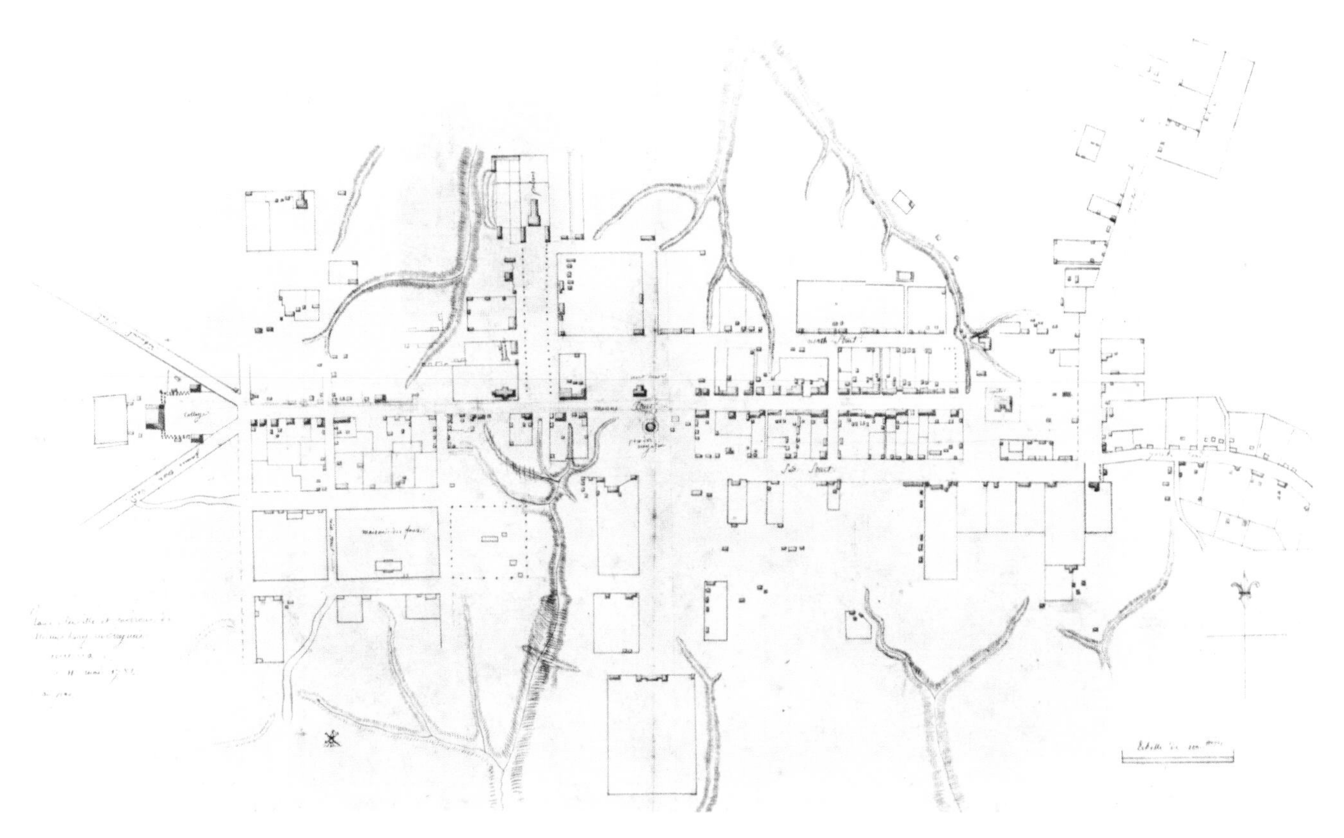

*Determining the location and size of colonial Williamsburg's many buildings was facilitated by what has become known as the "Frenchman's Map." The map, which was drawn in 1782, is thought to have been an aid in the billeting of French soldiers in Williamsburg during 1782 after the defeat of British forces at Yorktown in 1781.*

*The Association for the Preservation of Virginia Antiquities (APVA) came to the rescue of the deteriorating Powder Magazine. The motive was simply to stop further loss of historic landmarks, but with the magazine it felt compelled to make some attempt at restoration because of the bad condition. Missing bricks were replaced, and funds were raised for two stained glass memorial windows, one to Governor Alexander Spotswood, and one to Nathaniel Bacon. In this form the magazine became a tiny museum with admission tickets priced at ten cents. APVA still retains ownership of the Powder Magazine for which it paid six hundred dollars; the association leased it to The Colonial Williamsburg Foundation.*

*This windmill near Nicholson Street in restored Williamsburg is a reconstruction, but the mill is identical to the eighteenth-century structure owned by William Robertson.*

*The construction in Williamsburg of a hospital for mental patients was authorized by the General Assembly in 1769, and the Virginia Lunatic Asylum was completed in 1773. From the beginning of the hospital, the first mental institution in the United States, persons unable to pay were treated free of charge. The first building was on an eight-acre site on Francis Street, but in 1970 the facility was moved to a much larger location west of Williamsburg. This engraving depicts the institution about 1845.*

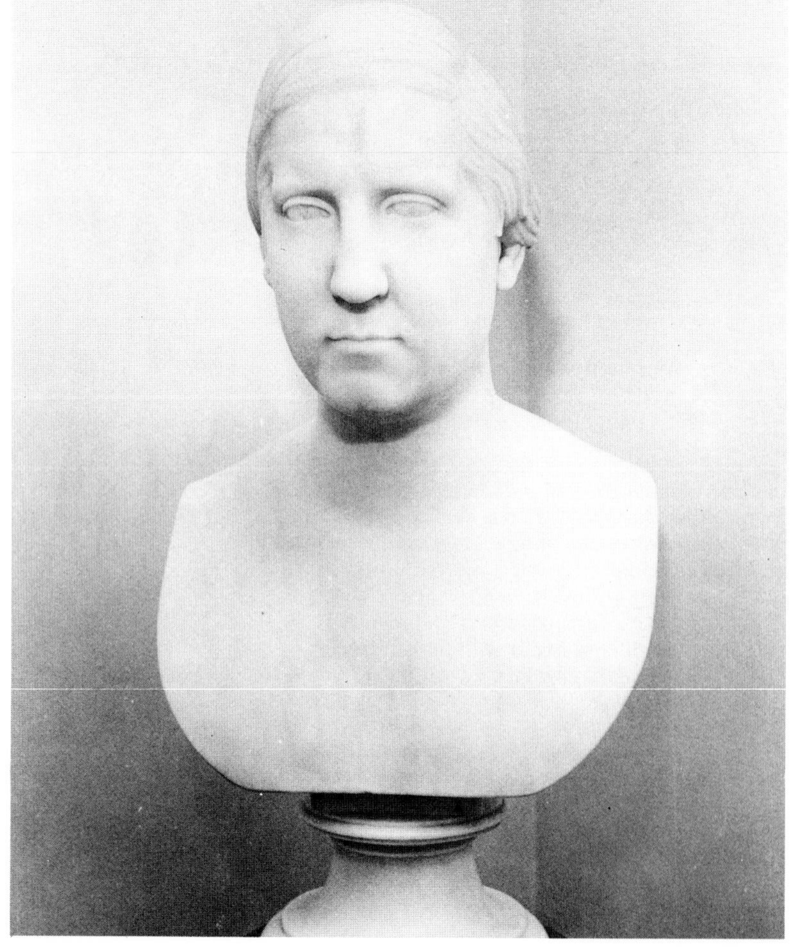

*This old sketch, from the files at Eastern State Hospital library, seems to indicate that additional building had extended the complex beyond the 1845 rendition.*

*This meticulous model of the original Virginia Lunatic Asylum is on display in the lobby of the main building, along with a bust of Dr. John M. Galt II, who was the first medical superintendent, a post created by an act of the legislature in 1841. When Galt came to the job in July of that year, he was only twenty-two. Patients then numbered 125. The count in January 1979 was 1,367. Starting with his grandfather, the first Dr. John M. Galt, who was also a vestryman at Bruton Parish and on the board of directors for the College of William and Mary, the patients were in the care of the Galt family for nearly a hundred years.*

*An old Williamsburg scrapbook yields a view of a street running "from the asylum to the present location of the Williamsburg Lodge" and a picture of a "well-known patient."*

*The windowless kitchen at Eastern State Hospital is a far cry from today's modern facility.*

*The Galt house, one of the oldest in Williamsburg, was first built by William Robertson before 1718. Later it was the residence of the Nelsons, including Thomas, a signer of the Declaration of Independence. Sold to the Galt family in 1823, the house has been occupied by descendants of that family ever since.*

*The value of advertising was certainly not lost to the proprietor of this Williamsburg garage in the early 1900s. The structure, which was a store operated by Prentis & Company in the 1700s, has now been restored to its eighteenth-century appearance and offers for sale items handcrafted for The Colonial Williamsburg Foundation.*

*A turn-of-the-century view of the Colonial Hotel shows dirt streets and a horse-drawn wagon. It was boasted in the 1890s that the inn could house a hundred guests.*

*By 1918 Duke of Gloucester Street was divided by a narrow median into two paved lanes, and automobiles had come to Williamsburg. This street was the original site of the Raleigh Tavern.*

*Spread in all its Victorian splendor along Duke of Gloucester Street, the Colonial Hotel was an impressive site in 1920. But the hotel occupied the site of Chowning's Tavern, and it was removed to make way for a reminder of an earlier age.*

*Never mind that their forebears had indulged in bowling on the Palace Green and elsewhere; as Williamsburg made its way into the 1890s, baseball found its way into Williamsburg. An early snapshot shows little action, but a lot of style at homeplate.*

*Mrs. Hobson, who lived in Wythe House, posed with her boarders in the summer of 1875. They were mostly College of William and Mary students.*

*These photographs of Duke of Gloucester Street in the 1890s indicate the rather sleepy state of affairs that existed in the town during the late nineteenth century. The College of William and Mary had reopened after its difficulties following the Civil War, and the lunatic asylum remained open, but the town rested quietly until restoration efforts were begun in 1926.*

*Despite the abundance of taverns in colonial Williamsburg, the Raleigh Tavern was the social, commercial, and political center of the colony. The original tavern burned in 1859, and this series of photographs shows the foundations of the historic structure and the rebuilt tavern with its famous Apollo Room. The tavern was dedicated to Sir Walter Raleigh, and the Apollo Room was the scene of great banquets; meetings of leaders such as Patrick Henry, Thomas Jefferson, and George Washington, and the founding of the scholarly society Phi Beta Kappa.*

*Motorcycles apparently enjoyed some popularity on Williamsburg streets, but one resident is evidently dubious as he watches a motor bike make its way past his property.*

*Another daring young woman of the time, from a photo found unidentified in an old scrapbook, is riding a motorcycle with a sidecar. Daring in more ways than one, she is wearing what appears to be a sailor suit complete with slacks.*

*Wheels. . . and more wheels! The Macon sisters pose with the Reverend Jones and his bicycle in the early 1900s. Modestly, the rider is attempting a sidesaddle mount.*

*"For my brother on his birthday," November 22, 1868, reads the inscription on the back of a tiny photograph of the demure Elizabeth Beverley Coleman.*

*Members of the Theta Delta Chi fraternity pose in 1917; Thomas G. Pullen, seated at left, for whom a research room is named at the college's Swem Library, later became principal of Hampton High School and head of the English department at nearby Newport News High School.*

*Elizabeth Macon and Margaret Tyler posed on Duke of Gloucester street in 1917 or 1918. It would be several years before the community would be the subject of thousands of tourist cameras. These young ladies, with their box Brownie, were intent only on photographing each other.*

*Most of the old photographs of Williamsburg families are contrived studio pictures or early snapshots that found their way into now-aging albums. Once in a while, however, an early "traveling photographer" would make his way to a Williamsburg home, and the end result would be a charming candid record such as this one. They are, left to right, Janet, Cynthia, and their mother, Mrs. George Coleman. Janet, now Dr. Kimbrough, lives in the St. George Tucker house in which this picture was made.*

*As photography became a part of family record keeping, backyard scenes such as this one, showing Mrs. Morecock and a group of young ladies, became regular events in Williamsburg and elsewhere.*

*Virginia Rona Davis, daughter of Lemuel Tyler Davis and Jennie Russell Davis, was a fashionable young lady when she posed for this turn-of-the-century photograph. The women of this supposedly "sleepy little community" did not lack for style.*

*Although uniforms have changed, the game was much the same, and these College of William and Mary students played basketball well. In fact, this group comprised a championship team in 1916. One of the reasons for its success was Henry M. Stryker, third from left, who would later be mayor of Williamsburg.*

*One of the highlights of the 1922 school year at the College of William and Mary was a visit by President Warren G. Harding. Harding, center, received a doctor of laws degree from Dr. James H. Dillard, rector of the college's board of visitors. While in Virginia's "historic triangle" Harding visited Yorktown and delivered an address at the Victory Monument concerning unity with Great Britain.*

*The first women admitted as students to the College of William and Mary were few in number. This group, wearing flowing garments for an aesthetic dance class, posed on the campus prior to 1921.*

*One of the most interesting student organizations at the College of William and Mary was the Walking Stick Club, strictly a social club. Some of the members posed in 1922 with, what else, their walking sticks. The club's motto: "If wishes were horses, beggars would ride"; its flower: "Virginia Creeper"; its song: "Tramp, Tramp, Tramp, etc." On those occasions when Mrs. George Coleman would lend them her car, the girls would take bacon and eggs and head for the "pond" (Matoaka Lake), where they would prepare breakfast.*

*In the so-called sleepy days of long-ago Williamsburg, two little boys are pictured on their way to school. Their ride was probably more fun than today's school bus.*

*Lucky are the children who share their lives with animals. Two ponies bring smiles to the faces of, left to right, Ben, Liela, Bee, Jimmy, and Oscar in this old snapshot. One youngster is unidentified.*

*Huge bouquets and skirts made of fabric petals made this group of bridesmaids in a 1928 Williamsburg wedding something to behold. The bride, in the fashion of the year, wore a short wedding gown.*

*Duke of Gloucester Street could have been mistaken for an average street in any one of thousands of small towns across the United States in 1928. But if a casual glance gave way to a careful look, signs of the town's historical importance were everywhere.*

*This series of photographs illustrates the changing appearance of the John Blair House on Duke of Gloucester Street in Williamsburg. It also gives the viewer an idea of how dramatically restoration changed the appearance of Williamsburg's historic area. The first photograph was made in the 1920s before restoration; the second depicts work on the house in the 1930s; the third shows the house after completion, and the fourth illustrates the kitchen, one of several outbuildings reconstructed on original foundations around the house. John Blair, Jr., lived in the house in the colonial period, and he had to fill the shoes of some rather prominent relatives. His grandfather Archibald's brother was the Reverend James Blair, and his father served twice as acting governor of Virginia. But John Blair, Jr., built a distinguished career, which included representing Virginia at the Constitutional Convention and being appointed to the U.S. Supreme Court by President George Washington. The buildings are privately occupied today.*

*The re-creation of colonial Williamsburg has been accomplished by hundreds of persons with diverse talents, but the dream was provided by the Reverend William Archer Rutherfoord Goodwin, and the money came from John D. Rockefeller, Jr. In this photograph, Goodwin, left, and Rockefeller are superimposed on plans for the restoration of Williamsburg.*

*Putting together enough information to rebuild colonial Williamsburg was much like assembling the pieces of a difficult puzzle. Of tremendous help to The Colonial Williamsburg Foundation historians was this engraving found in the Bodleian Library at Oxford University in England. The "Bodleian Plate" revealed precious information about the original buildings. The top panel shows the College of William and Mary; the center panel shows the Capitol Building and Governor's Palace; the bottom panel apparently shows local flora and fauna.*

*Despite their many differences, American colleges tend to share some characteristics; the celebration of homecoming is one of them. These photographs present two scenes from the College of William and Mary's 1934 homecoming day parade. The marching students indicate that the popularity of women's athletics is not a contemporary phenomenon. Even archery is represented in the parade.*

*Charles Washington Coleman, posing with his sash in April 1867, grew up to be a librarian at the College of William and Mary and then, later, a librarian at the Library of Congress.*

*Henry "Doc" Billups checks his watch to see if it's time to ring the bell at the College of William and Mary. By the time Billups died in 1955 he had become a legendary figure at the college. He rang the Wren Building bell for sixty-five years, served as a janitor, and shared his famous personality with thousands of students. The mutual affection between Billups and "his boys" led to his being honored by a chauffeured convertible in homecoming parades.*

*Dr. Earl G. Swem, who died in 1965, was librarian emeritus at the College of William and Mary until 1944. Dr. Swem, for whom the college library is named, was librarian for twenty-two years; he also became Virginia's leading bibliographer and edited numerous books and manuscripts on Virginia history.*

*Kippy and Eugene share childhood confidences in a Williamsburg backyard in 1934.*

*This 1938 photograph shows Mr. and Mrs. John D. Rockefeller, Jr., leaving Matthew Whaley School in Williamsburg. They attended a ceremony during which a portrait of Rockefeller by Robert Brackman was unveiled. The painting was commissioned by the citizens of Williamsburg as a tribute to the benefactor of the town's restoration. To their right can be seen George P. Coleman, for whom Coleman Memorial Bridge at Yorktown was named. A Williamsburg resident, Coleman was a Virginia highway commissioner and an important contributor to state and national highway development.*

*Mr. and Mrs. John D. Rockefeller, Jr., began collecting folk art in the 1920s, and Mrs. Rockefeller loaned part of her collection to The Colonial Williamsburg Foundation in 1935. In 1939, Abby Rockefeller decided to give the collection to the foundation, and her husband donated funds to construct and maintain this handsome brick home for the collection, which became the Abby Aldrich Rockefeller Folk Art Center in Williamsburg. The home and its fountain, which sparkles in the winter moonlight, are visited each year by thousands of persons who are interested in objects indigenous to American culture.*

*Dignitaries attending ceremonies at the College of William and Mary in 1954 pose with a bust of John Marshall, unveiled during the program. They are, left to right, Lord Goddard, Lord Chief Justice of England; the Honorable Earl Warren, Chief Justice of the United States; Mrs. A. I. Dupont, and Alvin Duke Chandler, then president of the college. Lord Goddard convulsed his captive audience by presenting his entire address in Latin.*

*Sam Mathews has a reason to smile. He won Williamsburg's "fishing rodeo" in August 1954 by catching the smallest fish. He is congratulated by the town's mayor, Dr. Henry M. Stryker. A dentist who died in 1974, Stryker was mayor for twenty years. A much-honored resident of the town, he had attended the College of William and Mary.*

*Fannie Lou Stryker of Williamsburg and Shirley Temple Black held a reunion in August 1976. When they first met in 1938, Mrs. Stryker was a hostess who guided the then-child movie star around the town's historic area. On this visit, Mrs. Black, U.S. Chief of Protocol, was accompanying the President of Finland around colonial Williamsburg. Mrs. Stryker is the widow of Dr. Henry M. Stryker, long-time mayor of Williamsburg.*

*Freshmen at the College of William and Mary humbly paid their respects to Botetourt Statue in 1957. Paying homage to the statue in front of the Wren Building was a tradition until the monument was moved into the library. The statue honors Norborne Berkeley, Baron de Botetourt, one of Virginia's most popular governors, who was appointed governor-general in August 1768.*

*Left to right: Gerald Ford, colonial Williamsburg militia master Nick Payne, and Katherine Godwin, wife of former Virginia Governor Mills Godwin.*

*The historic triangle, birthplace of many of America's colonial leaders, has welcomed distinguished modern leaders as well. In 1948 presidential candidate Harry S Truman met with Virginia Governor William Tuck.*

*Dwight D. Eisenhower visited the College of William and Mary in May 1953. He came to address the graduating class and traveled via presidential yacht to a spot not far from the colonial capital.*

*Lyndon B. Johnson, left, attended a meeting of Associated Press managing editors after being elected vice president to John F. Kennedy in 1960. He left Williamsburg and flew immediately overseas on a fact-finding mission for the new administration.*

*In October 1968, Richard M. Nixon campaigned in the Great Hall in the Wren Building.*

*President Jimmy Carter, right, chats with Henry Howell in Williamsburg, September 1977.*

*With the sun just right on a winter afternoon, light seems to explode on a window of the Courthouse of 1770 in Williamsburg's historic area. The restored courthouse, originally constructed in 1770, dramatizes the precept of rule by law, which has stood as a foundation of the country's political system. Both the local and James City County courts met in the courthouse until the 1930s. Noncapital criminal cases and some civil cases were decided in the courts, and important public notices were posted near the door of the building.*

*Members of this eighteenth-century dance group in Williamsburg are practicing for a ball and illustrating a favorite entertainment of colonial Virginians. The dance might be a stately minuet, a quadrille, a jig, or a reel. Dancers were accompanied by live music provided mainly by local performers. The colonies also imported instructors, who provided Virginians with lessons in the latest European dance steps.*

*These carolers are only one feature of what has become known as the Williamsburg Christmas. Each year the town is bathed in the warm glow of candlelight and colonial celebration. Several homes are opened for touring, and sightseers can gaze at antiques and enjoy the decorations that re-create Christmas in the colony.*

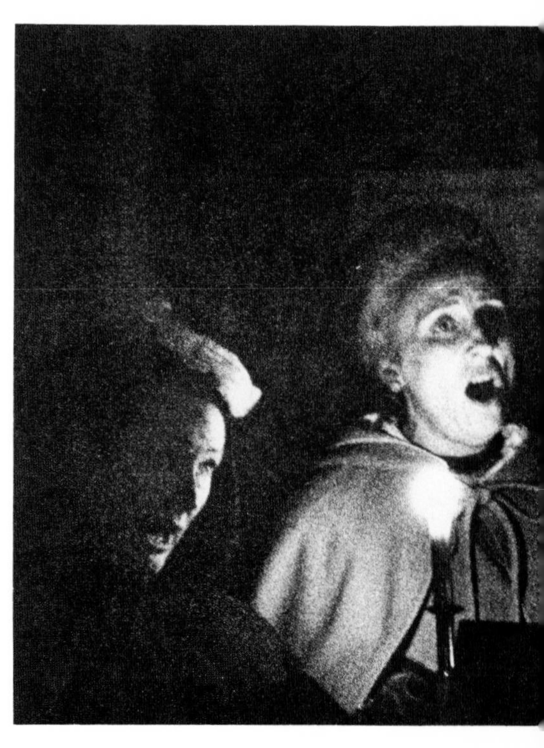

*A picture of Casey's father and a brother hangs on the wall in a house on Richmond Road. Casey, even now, says, "I don't object to progress or changing times."*

*Carleton Casey is, at ninety-six, Williamsburg's oldest living native son. At ninety-two, when this photograph was made, his appearance belied his age. He remembers the area before sidewalks and paved streets and grew up when "the city stopped at the college gates." His father established a grocery store and later expanded with a dry goods and notions store in the family living room. Eventually the corner where the present-day Casey's stands was obtained, and when it was sold to new owners, they asked to retain the name.*

*Duke of Gloucester Street runs through Merchants Square in Williamsburg. The area, which is closed to vehicular traffic, contains shops constructed in colonial style and is the commercial center of the re-created colonial capital. At the end of the street is the campus of the College of William and Mary.*

*A couple of sightseers visiting Williamsburg's historic area in 1977 take advantage of a convenient bench facing one of the town's many gardens before continuing their exploration. Residents and visitors to Williamsburg in the 1700s also found the town's many gardens attractive, and strolling among them was a favorite colonial entertainment.*

*People from all over the world visit the restored colonial Williamsburg for a look at American history. They also receive a taste of southern hospitality, preserved at such facilities as the Williamsburg Inn. The inn, illustrated by a photograph in 1937 that shows workers cleaning up the area after its construction, and also in a contemporary photograph, is owned and operated by The Colonial Williamsburg Foundation. The inn and its satellite facilities provide accommodations and famous foods to thousands of patrons each year.*

*"The Common Glory," an outdoor drama that was a popular Williamsburg attraction, was performed for the last time in 1976. The play about the early days of the American Revolution was presented at the Lake Matoaka Amphitheater for almost thirty years. Its opening performance was July 17, 1947. Written by Paul Green and directed by Howard Scammon, it brought history alive as actors and dancers performed on a stage built on the edge of the lake. The magic that started with a walk through the woods to reach the theater and culminated in the beautiful costumes and vivid reenactment of revolutionary times, became a tradition lasting until our bicentennial year. After rising costs brought about its demise, the theater was turned over to the College of William and Mary.*

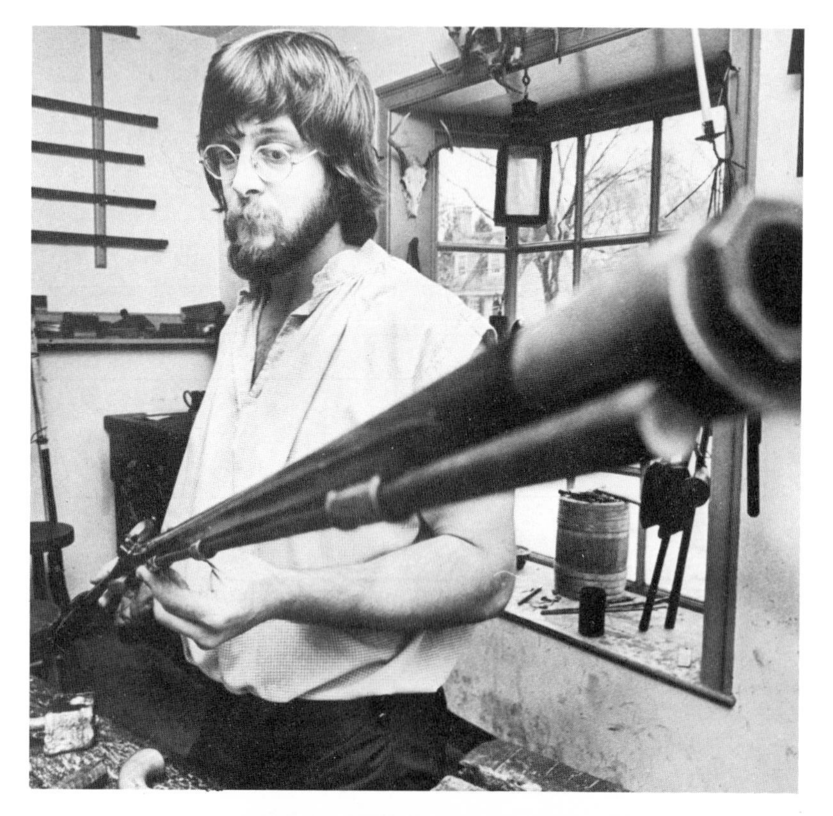

*Dozens of contemporary artisans and interpretive specialists keep alive the tools of their ancestors' trades in the restored colonial capital. In these photographs a gunsmith, silversmith, and leather workers demonstrate the technology of the 1700s. The reconstructed Deane Shop and Forge on Prince George Street encompasses two craft houses operated by The Colonial Williamsburg Foundation.*

DEANE
SHOP
AND
FORGE

*The visitor to Williamsburg takes a giant step into American history. The buildings and gardens create an ambiance of old that entertains and educates, while the people of the restored colonial capital breathe life into the landscape. Hundreds of highly trained people work in period costumes. Whether they're militiamen mustering and marching or guides assisting visitors through the many buildings on display, the people of The Colonial Williamsburg Foundation help transport visitors to the sense of a living heritage.*

*One more attraction was added in the area with the opening in May 1975 of Busch Garden's theme park, "the Old Country." An amusement park on the grand scale, it offers performances, animals, Old World atmosphere, and thrilling rides. The latest of these, the Loch Ness Monster, opened in 1978 with Governor John Dalton joining August Busch in the initial pass over the park.*

*The Colonial Parkway near Yorktown.*

# Yorktown

Like a Roman candle with successive illuminating bursts, each town in Virginia's historic triangle rose to prominence, and as it began to fade in importance, was replaced by another. Yorktown, which rivaled Williamsburg in stature early in the eighteenth century, was reduced to a small village by the time the capital of Virginia was moved from Williamsburg in 1780. But Yorktown's glory was yet to come.

A Frenchman, Nicolas Martiau, was the first person to be granted land in the Yorktown area. Around 1630 homes began appearing, and there was a ferry at the location of Yorktown before 1691. The site was originally in Charles River County when the colony was divided into eight counties in 1634. In 1642, when named York, the county consisted of several plantations, but the area was slow to be settled because of Indian hostility.

When tobacco became Virginia's main industry, the need for shipping points increased. In 1691 the Act for Ports became law, and the General Assembly ordered "that the court on the 29th day of this instant July meet upon Mr. Benjamin Reade's land, beginning at the lower side of Smyth's Creek, and so running downward by the river towards the ferry being ye land appointed by law for a port, in order to laying out of the same for a town and doing all other things related thereto, and that the sheriff give notice to the surveyor of this county that he then and there give his attendance." The act was passed to establish fifteen ports, so that Great Britain could ensure it received the customs due from trade.

Colonel Lawrence Smith completed the survey for Yorktown in August 1691. The town was laid out in eighty-five half-acre lots. Main Street ran atop the steep bluff, parallel to the water, and seven streets intersected it. Later, Water Street, along the lower riverfront, was added as "common ground." The shore area—the location of the town's wharves and ferry and warehouses—remained "common ground" until 1788.

Joseph Ring and Lieutenant Thomas Ballard were

*The Swan Tavern in Yorktown is now an antique shop, but in colonial days it was a popular gathering place. Opened in 1722 by "Scotch Tom" Nelson and James Walker, the eighteenth-century tavern attracted planters, merchants, and sea captains with its whiskey, peach brandy, wine, and ale. Outside the tavern's door was posted the notice: "My liquor's good, my measures just, But, honest Sirs, I will not trust." The tavern on Main Street was destroyed when the courthouse exploded in the 1860s, but it was rebuilt in the 1930s by the National Park Service. The tavern's back door today is guarded by stone dogs, a recent embellishment placed there by an antique dealer.*

The Dudley Digges House is one of two surviving wood-frame houses that are believed to have existed in eighteenth century Yorktown. The dwelling, located at Main and Comte de Grasse streets, was restored during 1959 and 1960. The house is thought to have been built for Dudley Digges, Jr., a prominent citizen of Yorktown. The dependent structures —the granary, kitchen, and smokehouse— were rebuilt. The building is considered a typical mid-eighteenth-century house, with functional dependent units grouped in a plantation arrangement.

Yorktown was created for the collection of customs, and they were collected at this house built by Richard Ambler, the collector of customs, who had settled in Yorktown by 1720. The prosperous businessman had the house constructed at Main and Read streets in the early 1720s, and it became known as the "Old Customshouse." Ambler and his wife Elizabeth had three sons, and all served as customs agents. The Customshouse was acquired by the Comte de Grasse Chapter of the Daughters of the American Revolution in 1924 and was restored in 1930.

trustees of the new town, which was named for the Duke of York. Houses, businesses, and wharves appeared, and warehouses provided storage for hogsheads of tobacco that were rolled into town from nearby plantations.

Yorktown was so successful by the early 1700s that all of its lots were occupied. It was a thriving village and county seat: tall-masted sailing ships left with their holds full of tobacco, and ships sailed in laden with manufactured goods and finery so sought-after by residents of the colony. The town was also a debarkation point for many Africans who were sold as slaves, the necessary ingredient to make the tobacco industry thrive. Tobacco was so popular that it became legal tender in the colony.

Yorktown's apex was reached about 1750. It was a collage of colonists, aristocratic planters, ships' captains, common stevedores, and slaves who roamed the docks and busy streets of the port town. One of the favorite meeting

*Although Yorktown had declined dramatically by the Revolutionary War, dozens of houses and buildings remained in the 1750s. This view of Yorktown was probably drawn by one of the British officers of the crew of the HMS* Success *or HMS* Norwich, *which sailed to Virginia in 1754-56.*

*Thomas Nelson, Jr., signed the Declaration of Independence and commanded Virginia's militia during the siege of Yorktown.*

places and Yorktown's most popular spot for conversation and news was Swan Tavern, which opened in 1722 and served whiskey, rum, ale, cider, and hearty meals.

The busiest place was probably the Customshouse, built about 1721 by Richard Ambler, who was collector of customs in the early 1700s. The Customshouse was originally a storehouse, but it became the place where merchandise was weighed and measured and duties were paid on imports and exports. To this most important center in the settlement, captains came to pay their taxes, obtain sailing papers, and exchange gossip. They also must have discussed the many pirates who infested the Virginia Capes and became such a problem that ships waited in Hampton Roads until there were enough to sail in a convoy.

During the early 1700s Yorktown was port of entry for cities even in the North; thus customs collector Ambler, also a successful businessman, was an important figure in the colony. Perhaps the most notable Yorktown citizen during the early years was Thomas Nelson, Jr., whose father, "Scotch Tom" Nelson, was the first in a line of famous Nelsons. The senior Nelson became a successful businessman, and his heirs became political and military leaders. Thomas Nelson, Jr., signed the Declaration of Independence, led Virginia's militia during the siege of his hometown, and became governor of the state. He was financially ruined during the Revolutionary War because he supported the effort with his personal fortune.

The General Assembly directed that a courthouse be built in Yorktown, and in 1697 the courthouse, erected at a

cost of thirty thousand pounds of tobacco, was completed. A larger brick structure replaced it in 1733, but it burned in 1814.

Yorktown in its heyday was described by a visitor: "You perceive a great air of opulence amongst the inhabitants who have some of them built themselves houses, equal in magnificence to many of our superb ones at St. James [England]; the most considerable houses are of brick; some handsome ones of wood, all built in the modern taste; and the lessor sort, of plaster. There are some very pretty garden spots in the town; and the avenues leading to Williamsburg and Norfolk are prodigiously agreeable."

Even at its peak, Yorktown never had more than 2,500 residents, and the town had begun to suffer prior to the Revolutionary War due to the decline of tobacco. The war brought disruption of trade, and when shells began falling on the little village of about sixty houses and several public buildings, they were the final blow.

Nothing about the Virginia village suggested it would be the location of the greatest battle in the Revolutionary War. Residents had their own tea party in 1774, when they dumped two half-chests of tea into the York River to exhibit their distaste for English policies, but nothing of magnitude had taken place when a series of forces moved inexorably toward Yorktown.

General George Washington, who had prosecuted the war in the North for the most part, was in desperate need of a victory in 1781. Fortune favored him, however. Lieutenant General Charles Cornwallis, who was second in command of British forces in the colonies under Gen-

*By 1781 Yorktown was no longer the bustling port town it had been in the early 1700s. It suffered from the decline of tobacco and the disruption of trade that resulted from the American Revolution. This Sidney King painting illustrates Yorktown after the British moved their headquarters from Portsmouth, Virginia, to the small village on the York River.*

*Although many of Yorktown's structures survived the colonial period intact and others were rebuilt, the old windmill was lost during the intervening years. The tower, constructed in 1711, became one of the town's landmarks and was present during the siege of 1781. The windmill is illustrated by this print from the* Family Magazine, *New York edition, 1840.*

*One of the greatest heroes to emerge from the American Revolution was the Marquis de Lafayette. Although a Frenchman, Lafayette spent his time and personal fortune aiding Americans in their struggle for independence. Lafayette was in charge of the American force that confronted Lieutenant General Charles Cornwallis in Virginia. The French aristocrat, in his early twenties at the time of the siege, became a hero in the United States and France as well. After his return to France in 1782, Lafayette continued to champion the United States throughout his years as a political leader despite his preoccupation with the stormy political scene of his homeland.*

*Yorktown in 1781, depicted in this painting by Richard H. Janson at Yorktown Visitor Center, was a quiet village, but the ravages of the siege changed that. After the siege an American described the houses as "greatly damaged, and some totally ruined, being shot through in a thousand places and honey-combed, ready to crumble to pieces." The battle was a devastating blow to the town. Prior to the siege, Yorktown had about two thousand residents, but by 1790 only about 660 remained.*

*Lieutenant General Charles Cornwallis was second in command of British forces in the colonies. His southern campaign began with an invasion of North Carolina, and in 1781 Cornwallis brought his troops to Yorktown, where the Marquis de Lafayette watched his movements with a much smaller American force. The British general's surrender ended hopes for victory over the colonies and eventually led to a negotiated settlement of the conflict. Cornwallis' later career included the governorship of India.*

*Admiral Francois de Grasse played a dramatic role in defeating the British at Yorktown. The arrival of his fleet in Hampton Roads sealed off a possible British escape by sea, and the French admiral's fleet withstood an attack by a British fleet commanded by Rear Admiral Thomas Graves on September 5, 1781. The sea battle and subsequent withdrawal of the British fleet meant doom for the British and German soldiers at Yorktown. This painting of the admiral is displayed at the United States Naval Academy at Annapolis, Maryland.*

*George Washington, a native of Virginia, was a frequent visitor to Williamsburg and Yorktown during colonial times, but it was his 1781 trip to the historic triangle that proved crucial in the Revolutionary War. Washington's victory over Lieutenant General Charles Cornwallis at Yorktown was the culmination of leadership that prevailed over almost impossible circumstances. His military success and political leadership as President of the United States led to the familiar sobriquet "Father of his Country." This painting of Washington by Gilbert Stuart hangs in the Capitol Building in Williamsburg.*

*Fortunately for these members of the First Virginia Regiment, the smoke of battle is simulated. The regiment was encamped at Yorktown Victory Center in October 1976 for Yorktown Day festivities celebrating the 196th anniversary of the American victory, commemorated each year by wreath-layings, patriotic ceremonies and parades.*

*To take advantage of Lieutenant General Charles Cornwallis' decision to station his forces in Yorktown, and possibly to bottle up the British, General George Washington had to move his troops and the French from New York. This 1976 painting by artist Sidney King commissioned by* The Daily Press,Inc.*, shows Washington's troops resting at Endview Plantation in Newport News, Virginia, before moving on to Yorktown and beginning the siege that brought British surrender.*

*These contemporary Americans wear the types of uniforms and arms the British used in their defense of Yorktown. The most striking feature of the uniforms is their formal, decorative nature, more suited for show than for battle. About 7,500 British and German soldiers defended Yorktown. The Englishmen were all professional soldiers and the Germans were mercenaries.*

eral Henry Clinton, began his Virginia campaign in 1781. After playing a cat-and-mouse game with the Marquis de Lafayette, the young Frenchman who was commander of a much smaller force, Cornwallis moved his Virginia base of operations from Portsmouth, Virginia, to Yorktown. Clinton had ordered Cornwallis to find a site for a naval station, and British officials decided Portsmouth did not provide enough protection for their ships.

The only significant action between Cornwallis and Lafayette was a battle at Green Spring, near Jamestown—an engagement important only because Lafayette avoided a trap laid by the English general that would have been disastrous to American plans. It had been Lafayette's assignment to follow and hinder British activities, but to avoid a confrontation that would allow British superiority in numbers to destroy the American forces. Then, when Washington in New York received word that a sizeable French fleet under the command of Admiral Francois de Grasse was sailing from France toward the colonies, the pieces of an important puzzle began to fall into place.

Cornwallis and his troops, who had arrived in Yorktown and Gloucester (across the York River) on August 2, were encamped in Yorktown under the watchful eye of Lafayette. If de Grasse's fleet could arrive in the Chesa-

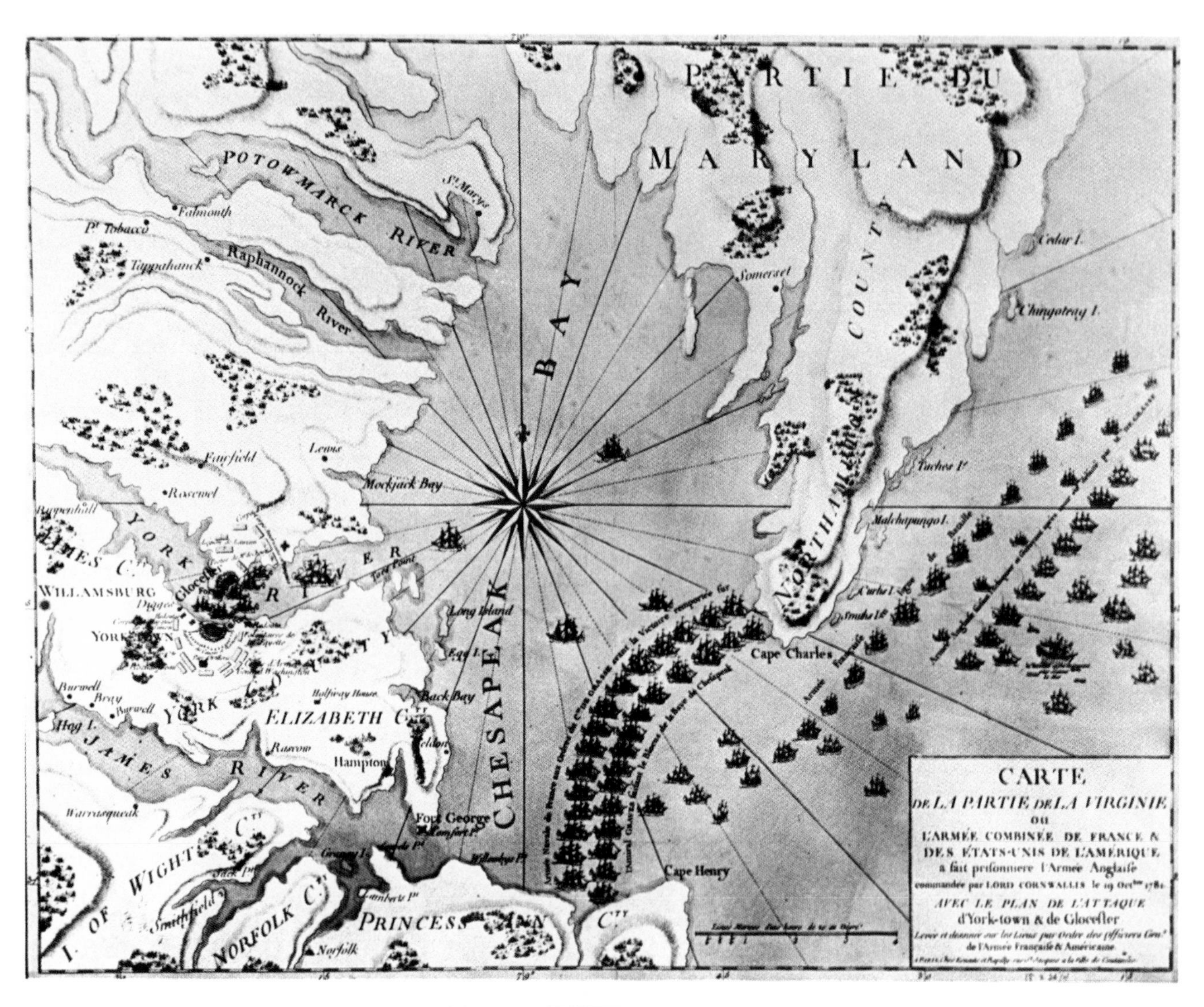


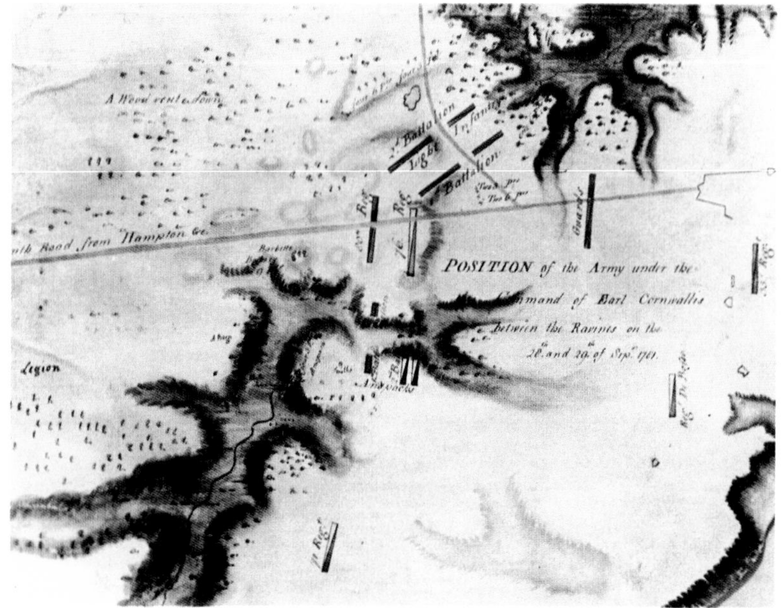


*A French chart of the lower Chesapeake Bay illustrates the hopeless position of the English when the French fleet arrived in Hampton Roads. The French blockade withstood an attempt by a British fleet under the command of Rear Admiral Thomas Graves to break through and aid the British ashore on September 5, 1781. The battle was a draw, but the French fleet remained between the army and the British fleet, creating the blockade which defeated the British army.*

*This pen-and-ink drawing depicts the positions of a portion of the army of Lieutenant General Charles Cornwallis at Yorktown on September 28 and 29 in 1781. When Cornwallis was led to believe he would be reinforced with troops dispatched by General Henry Clinton in New York, he abandoned his outer defense line, a move which greatly aided the American and French forces when they began their siege of the trapped British army.*

*The Sebastian Bauman map of 1781 shows Yorktown under siege and naval vessels in the York River. Both sides constructed extensive fortifications and trench work, with the British strongly fortified within the village. About thirty artillery pieces were trained on the British from the Grand French Battery, and the constant bombardment and tightening grip by the Americans and French brought about the British capitulation.*

peake Bay and if the American and French armies under Washington and Rochambeau could hurriedly reach Yorktown, there might be a plum for the picking. After analyzing the situation, Washington and Rochambeau began moving troops southward from New England on August 19, and Lafayette sealed off Cornwallis' escape route to the Carolinas.

When armies under the command of Washington and Rochambeau arrived on the Virginia peninsula after a well-executed but punishing march, Cornwallis' neck was in a noose. De Grasse's arrival with his twenty-four French warships tightened the hold.

Although Rear Admiral Thomas Graves brought a British fleet to intercept the French ships, the move failed to rescue Cornwallis. A sea battle began just after 4:15 p.m. on September 5 outside the Virginia Capes between the French ships and the nineteen British vessels. Although the French had the advantage, the battle, which

*Located under the bluffs along Yorktown's waterfront, "Cornwallis' Cave," according to legend, provided safety for British soliders from the cannon balls that fell on their fortifications and provided a safe place to store ammunition for the British, and later the Confederates during their occupation of Yorktown during the Civil War. Lieutenant General Charles Cornwallis is thought to have met in the cave with his officers when occupancy of the Nelson House became too dangerous.*

*The defensive fortifications so carefully constructed by the British proved less than successful against the Americans and French. These contemporary photographs provide an interesting view of fortifications, particularly a reconstructed redoubt (a defensive fortification) with fraises (sharpened timbers) to repel invaders. Redoubts Nine and Ten were in advance of the British defensive lines, and both were taken in 1781 in about thirty minutes of fighting.*

was over by 6:30 that evening, was indecisive. This worked to the advantage of the French, however, who remained between the British fleet and Englishmen stranded ashore. After waiting four days, the British ships returned to New York, and the English army was doomed to be strangled slowly by the allies' land and sea superiority.

The French fleet continued to control Chesapeake Bay, and the American and French armies began tightening their grip on land. Washington joined Lafayette at his headquarters in Williamsburg on September 14, and by the end of the month, the allies had more than fifteen thousand troops for the siege. They marched on Yorktown on September 28.

Both Yorktown and Gloucester Point had been fortified by British earthworks and batteries. When Cornwallis, who commanded about 7,500 English and German troops, received word that he would be reinforced by Clinton in New York, he withdrew from his outer defenses on September 29 and 30. This maneuver aided the allies, and they took the British outer defenses and strengthened them.

*The fury of hand-to-hand combat is especially vivid in this painting by Louis E. Lami of the storming of a British fortification at Yorktown. French and American troops had to conquer two redoubts the night of October 14 before a second siege line could be completed. They took them in a matter of minutes, and their stranglehold on the British tightened. This 1840 painting hangs in the old Senate chamber in Virginia's Capitol Building in Richmond.*

*The surrender terms for Lieutenant General Charles Cornwallis' army were drawn up by British, French, and American officers on October 18, 1781, in this room of the Moore House. Today, the historic room is open to the public as part of Colonial National Historical Park. Acquired by the National Park Service in 1931, the Moore House has been restored to its original colonial appearance and is furnished with period pieces. The structure, which dates from the early 1700s, was owned in 1781 by Augustine Moore, a prosperous Yorktown merchant.*

*Some signs of the siege's impact on Yorktown have remained throughout the years: two cannonballs are still lodged in the Nelson House. General Thomas Nelson, Jr., was commander of the Virginia militia during the siege. Supposedly, when asked where the French and Americans should direct their cannon fire, Nelson told them to aim for his house. The resident of Yorktown suspected that his house, the most elegant in the town, might be the headquarters of Lieutenant General Charles Cornwallis. Nelson's patriotism prevailed over his self-interest and led to his financial ruin.*

On the night of October 6 work was begun on the first siege line. Digging continued as the allies strengthened their positions and erected batteries to bombard the enemy. On October 9 the American and French armies opened fire, and for two days the English and German troops lived with the scream of shells overhead and with explosions all around them. But disease and illness were more devastating than the artillery duel. The allies sent their ailing soldiers fifteen miles away to Williamsburg, where they were hospitalized in the abandoned Governor's Palace. British forces were riddled with illness, too.

As the bombardment rose in intensity, the pressure mounted, and the death toll rose. The first siege line was established about eight hundred yards from the British

*A diorama at Colonial National Historical Park Yorktown Visitor Center re-creates the British army's march out of Yorktown on October 19, 1781. The English and German troops, led by Brigadier General Charles O'Hara, marched off to the tune of "The World Turned Upside Down." They traveled somberly between the French on one side and Americans on the other to Surrender Field, where they laid down their arms.*

defenses. On the night of October 11 a second siege line was begun, much closer to British positions. Redoubts Nine and Ten (defensive fortifications) had to be taken before the second parallel could be completed. Four hundred Frenchmen were assigned to attack Redoubt Nine, which was manned by about 120 English and German troops. They conquered the fortification in less than thirty minutes. Four hundred Americans, led by Alexander Hamilton, assaulted Redoubt Ten. It was held by about seventy defenders, who were overpowered in about ten minutes.

Cornwallis attempted to remove his army during the night of October 16, but bad weather prevented their crossing to Gloucester. So on October 17 he proposed a truce. Fourteen Articles of Capitulation for the surrender were worked out at the Moore House on October 18, and on October 19 the British army marched out of Yorktown to a tune played by the British band, "The World Turned

*This artist's conception of the surrender at Yorktown captures the solemnity of the occasion. Commander of the British troops, Lieutenant General Charles Cornwallis, pleaded illness and sent Brigadier General Charles O'Hara to surrender. Major General Benjamin Lincoln received the British general's sword, and General George Washington informed Congress that a reduction of the English army had been "most happily effected."*

*In this contemporary view, the tranquility of Surrender Field at Yorktown contrasts with the drama of its history. For at this site British and German soldiers and sailors stacked their weapons after Brigadier General Charles O'Hara surrendered his sword to American Major General Benjamin Lincoln. The surrender brought efforts by a new British cabinet to negotiate for peace.*

Upside Down." British and German troops marched between a long line of dazzlingly dressed French soldiers on one side and rag-tag Americans on the other. Cornwallis, pleading illness, remained at his headquarters, so Brigadier General Charles O'Hara presented his sword to Major General Benjamin Lincoln.

Although the Treaty of Paris ending hostilities between the colonies and Great Britain wasn't signed until 1783, the surrender of Cornwallis to American and French troops on October 19, 1781, was instrumental in freeing the American colonies.

The victory was invaluable to the colonies' cause, but it was costly for Yorktown. An American soldier described the havoc wreaked in the town by the allies' artillery: "I have this day visited the town of York, to witness the destructive effects of the siege. It contains about sixty houses, some of them elegant, many of them greatly damaged, and some totally ruined, being shot through in a thousand places and honeycombed, ready to crumble to pieces. Rich furniture and books were scattered over the ground, and the carcasses of men and horses half covered the earth, exhibiting a scene of ruin and horror beyond description."

*The boom of cannon fire again resounded over Yorktown in 1862 during the Virginia peninsula campaign. Confederate General John B. Magruder was in charge of defending the peninsula against Union forces attempting to use the area as an approach to Richmond. The left flank of his defense line was anchored at Yorktown. General Joseph E. Johnston replaced Magruder, and Union General George B. McClellan began a siege of the Confederate positions. On May 4, Johnston retreated to another defense line a mile east of Williamsburg, where a battle led the Confederates to withdraw to Richmond. This illustration from the April 26, 1862* Harper's Weekly *shows an exchange between the Confederates occupying Yorktown and attacking Union troops.*

Few colonists learned as well as Yorktown's residents what freedom can cost. As news of the great victory spread throughout the colonies, Yorktown residents returned to the scene of "ruin and horror beyond description" to begin picking up the pieces. But even after the wounds of war began to heal, the settlement slipped into a state of somnolence. Prior to the siege Yorktown had about 2,300 residents, but in 1790 only about 660 remained. In 1814 a fire on the waterfront almost wiped out what was left of the town, and it destroyed many of Yorktown's original buildings.

When war again came to Virginia, it brought more devastation to Yorktown. During the Civil War, fortifications were established by Confederate soldiers in anticipation of a Union invasion led by General McClellan in the Virginia peninsula campaign. Confederate troops were commanded by General John B. Magruder, who had about 15,000 men at Yorktown, until reinforcements increased his army to about 36,000 soldiers. After Magruder was replaced by the Confederate General Johnston, the Rebels were besieged by Union forces and abandoned Yorktown and Norfolk in 1862. Yorktown was occupied by federal troops for the remainder of the war, and two

U.S. NATIONAL CEMETERY
ESTABLISHED 1866

For twenty-nine days in the Spring of 1862, Yorktown was visited by another siege. In this second year of the Civil War a Union army driving on Richmond was temporarily stalled by a thin Confederate line. Dead of both sides lie here.

*Although Yorktown's place in military history is almost exclusively tied to the Revolutionary War, it is also the site of a two-and-one-half acre cemetery for Civil War dead. The brick-enclosed cemetery with small, white stones to mark the graves contains the remains of more than two thousand soldiers. Established in 1866, the cemetery contains mostly Union remains, and some of the soldiers have been moved from as far away as fifty miles for interment at Yorktown. Although national cemeteries were designated for Union soldiers only, some of the dead at Yorktown were Confederates.*

casualties of occupation were the courthouse and Swan Tavern. Used to store ammunition, the courthouse blew up in 1863, and the explosion was of such magnitude that it destroyed the Swan Tavern across the street.

When next Yorktown was invaded, it was not during a war. The Federal Centennial Commission created a three-day program in 1881 to celebrate the Revolutionary War victory in Yorktown. The one hundredth anniversary, which lasted October 18 through 20, was celebrated by about 50,000 people. A highlight of the event was a speech by President Chester A. Arthur, who spoke to an array of dignitaries—from senators, congressmen and governors from all over the country to descendants of such Revolutionary War leaders as Rochambeau and Von Steuben. The small town was a crush of milling people, housed in a makeshift city of tents. The crowds and confusion prompted one disgruntled critic to remark, "The greatest mistake was in making Cornwallis surrender the place; he certainly should have kept it."

Centennial crowds, however, were nothing compared to the two hundred to three hundred thousand people who arrived in 1931 to celebrate the sesquicenten-

*Yorktown was fortified by Confederates during the Civil War to preclude a Union march up the peninsula to capture Richmond, the capital of the Confederacy. The Confederates abandoned their first line of defense in 1862, and Union troops occupied Yorktown for the remainder of the war. These photographs by Civil War photographer Mathew Brady illustrate the small town on the York River in 1862. They depict the buildup of ordnance, two Union soldiers at "Cornwallis' Cave," and an exploded gun at an abandoned Confederate battery.*

nial. Dignitaries for the celebration included President Herbert Hoover and Field Marshal Henri Petain. In typically American fashion, the festival was larger and longer, lasting October 16 through 19. Fireworks, band concerts, a pageant, and plenty of speeches filled the town.

Contemporary Yorktown no longer is the scene of rolling hogsheads of tobacco along its wharfs. Planters and merchants have been replaced by visitors who come from all over the world to see what remains of Yorktown's colonial greatness and where British plans for colonization were turned upside down by ragged, poorly armed men. Despite its fame, Yorktown has remained a small community. A few restaurants and shops on Water and Nelson streets, public buildings, and lovely residences comprise the town of about 350 persons.

The role Yorktown played in the American Revolution is the focus of two centers, Colonial National Historical Park Yorktown Visitor Center and the Yorktown Victory Center. The visitor center, which was renovated in 1976, is located on the battlefield. It has observation points that overlook the battlefield, displays of historical relics, a partial replica of an eighteenth-century frigate, and a driving tour of historical vantage points.

*In these views of Yorktown in 1881, the village's rural character is obvious, and the town looks surprisingly peaceful when one considers that the centennial celebration was held in that year and brought thousands of visitors to the village to take part in the festivities. But for the observers on the porch of the Yorktown Hotel, which fronted on Main Street, it was business, or lack of it, as usual along the dirt streets.*

The victory center, which opened in April 1976, is the largest of three bicentennial information centers that were built in Virginia. The facility houses exhibits that depict the course of the American Revolution, a museum of Revolutionary War artifacts, and tourist information. The victory center is located on about twenty-two acres of land overlooking the York River.

Despite the devastation and ruin that periodically struck Yorktown, the town still is rich in history, and like Jamestown and Williamsburg, its historic wealth has been preserved by people concerned about its past.

The National Park Service, which manages the historic park, rebuilt Swan Tavern in 1935 and has reconstructed other structures as well. The Customshouse, acquired by Comte de Grasse Chapter, Daughters of the American Revolution, has been restored, and Yorktown was named an official state historic landmark and placed on the National Register of Historic Places in 1973.

Many original houses, dating from the 1700s, provide examples of the beauty and practicality of Yorktown homes. The Moore House, where the Articles of Capitulation were drafted, is now exhibited by the National Park Service. During the summer months, costumed eigh-

*An illustration from* Harpers Weekly *of October 29, 1881, provides a view of the attractions at Yorktown's centennial celebration from October 18 through October 20, 1881. About twenty thousand people arrived in the town for the festivities, and the crowds far exceeded Yorktown's ability to handle them.*

*Although plans for construction of a Victory Monument at Yorktown were formulated in 1781, it took more than one hundred years before the marble column was erected. This photograph, taken during the October 18, 1881, centennial celebration, shows the laying of the cornerstone on a bluff overlooking the York River. The monument was completed in 1883, and the first of several Victory figures later was placed on top.*

*In October 1781, when Congress heard of the surrender of the British at Yorktown, it approved a monument to commemorate the event, but one hundred years passed before placement of the monument began. About a decade after the monument was started, the first Victory figure was placed atop the shaft. In 1942 Victory's head and arms were sheared off by a bolt of lightning, and Congress later approved a replacement figure. This figure, her arms outstretched in benediction, has a lightning rod running down to her feet to avoid the sad fate of her predecessor.*

teenth century officers of the French, American, and British armies give their accounts of the meeting and surrender terms. The Moore House serves as a reminder that a nation's will to be free can be more powerful than all the guns of an empire. ■

*The rustic nature of Yorktown in the early twentieth century is conveyed by this photograph of the Customshouse before it was restored in 1930. The Yorktown women visiting on the side porch don't seem greatly affected by the summer heat. Dirt roads and picket fences were common in the tranquil town before renovation returned much of it to its colonial appearance.*

*This man is taking advantage of low-cost transportation around the turn of the century, and he apparently has Yorktown's Main Street all to himself. The view is toward downtown Yorktown from Main and Nelson streets. The Nelson House stands just behind the trees on the left.*

*This view of Read Street in Yorktown in the early 1900s is toward Main Street. The Nelson House garden wall is on the right. The Blow family, who in the twentieth century acquired much of the village, enclosed several houses, including the Nelson House, within its bounds until the entire group was purchased by the National Park Service in 1968. Restoration was begun on the historic buildings in 1974 and was completed in 1976.*

GRACE EP ISC OPAL
ERECTED PRIOR TO 1700
BURNED BY THE ENG LISH NAVY IN 1814
REBUILT IN 1825 RESTORED IN 1920
NOW IN USE WAS M ADE IN 1725 AND WAS
PRESEN TO THE C HURCH BY
COMMUNION SILVER IS
STILL IN USE.
GEN. THOMAS NELSON JR. S
OF INDEPENDENCE IS BURI

*The first Grace Episcopal Church in Yorktown was built of marl slabs taken from the York River. Governor Francis Nicholson offered twenty pounds of sterling toward its construction with the stipulation that it be completed within two years. Lieutenant General Charles Cornwallis used the church as a powder magazine during the Revolutionary War. Burned during the 1814 fire, except for the thick marl walls, it was rebuilt in 1848 and restored in 1926. Among those buried in its graveyard is General Thomas Nelson, Jr.*

*Summers were peaceful when Williamsburg residents took off for Yorktown and the river. "Janet and Aunt Bettie" were deep in conversation when this picture was made. Aunt Bettie learned to read her Bible when she was in her late sixties.*

*A whale was the attraction on another occasion, when it washed up near the mouth of the York River. Two dozen men promptly rolled up their pants and posed in front of it. Curiously, they leave us a humorous, if leggy, recollection of the day, but they managed to totally obscure the whale.*

*A faded photograph shows a picnic in Yorktown held, incredibly, on March 16, 1895. Yorktown is cold in March, but something prompted this well-dressed group of ladies and gentlemen to pack a picnic basket and a blanket and head toward the York River.*

*Members of the Civilian Conservation Commission helped excavate at a French battery in the early 1930s and are shown digging on the second siege line constructed by the American and French forces at Yorktown in order to move closer to the British lines during the siege. Excavation sometimes produced surprising results, as in this view of a trench in the Fusiliers Redoubt. The skeletons are probably the remains of British soldiers.*

*One York County resident who remembered the Yorktown sesquicentennial of 1931, remarked, "I'm sure it was bigger than the planners ever thought it would be." Thousands of people visited Yorktown between October 16 and 19. Each of the original thirteen colonies sent representatives to put on pageants. Other entertainment included military drills, bands, and a reenactment of the historic battle. The stands, encampment, and visiting fleet are visible in this aerial photograph.*

*This aerial photograph of Yorktown in June 1931 provides a panoramic view of the village a few months before the sesquicentennial celebration of 1931. The Victory Monument is in the center of the photograph, and Main Street runs to the left of the monument. At the top of the photograph and at the bottom right can be seen portions of the York River.*

*Among the speakers at the 1931 sesquicentennial were President Herbert Hoover, General John J. Pershing, and Marshall Henri Petain of France. Hoover, shown here, delivered his speech on the third day to overflowing stands that were constructed on the battlefield.*

*In 1931 the Huguenot Society of Pennsylvania, in cooperation with the National Federation of Huguenot Societies and the Yorktown Sesquicentennial Commission, placed a monument to Nicolas Martiau on the site of his home. Martiau, the adventurous Huguenot who was born in France in 1591, came to Virginia in 1620. Through the marriage of his daughter Elizabeth to Colonal George Reade, he became the earliest American ancestor of George Washington and Thomas Nelson.*

*Yorktown Naval Weapons Station traces its origins back to 1918, when the Navy bought 13,400 acres in York County as part of a project to mine the North Sea. Although World War I ended before the project could be carried out, the Naval Mine Depot was created, and it became the Naval Weapons Station in 1956. Today the facility arms ships in the Atlantic and Mediterranean fleets. These photographs show the base around World War II and in 1979.*

*When Yorktown was begun in 1691 there must have been something of a building boom, since lot sales were brisk. The community later grew as a port town. Although thousands of tourists come to Yorktown each year, the town has remained small and quiet. With only about 350 residents in the 1970s, Yorktown's flavor is captured by this 1976 photograph of a man pausing to study the York River in front of the town's hardware store.*

*York County's current courthouse has many antecedents. Court was first held in the area in 1633 at the home of Captain John Utie, then moved from house to house until the home of Captain Robert Baldry was rented for a courthouse in 1658 for one thousand pounds of tobacco annually. The first courthouse building, a simple frame structure, was constructed in 1697 on the current site at Main and Ballard streets. It was replaced in 1733 by a brick structure which survived the Revolutionary War, but not a devastating fire in 1814. The courthouse was rebuilt in 1818 and was used as a powder magazine during the Civil War until it was destroyed by a gunpowder explosion in 1863 during Union occupancy. A fourth building, used from 1876 to 1940, also was destroyed by fire, and the present structure, shown here, was dedicated in 1955.*

*Going crabbing. Then, as now, gentlemen such as George P. Coleman found pleasure in discarding shoes in favor of boots and pursuing the not-so-elusive crab. All Tidewater shares Yorktown's passion for seafood.*

*Lieutenant General Charles Cornwallis would have had an easier time trying to evacuate his men across the York River to Gloucester Point if he had been able to use the George P. Coleman Memorial Bridge. Unfortunately for the British, the bridge didn't open until 1952. The structure shown here in 1976 is reportedly the largest double swing-span bridge in the world. The five-hundred-foot steel spans are designed to open ninety degrees simultaneously to provide a 450-foot clearance for ships, many of which are Navy vessels going up the York River to Yorktown Naval Weapons Station to take on ammunition.*

*This contemporary view of Yorktown in winter shows an almost deserted Main Street. The Thomas Pate House stands on the left. Built about 1700, the Pate House is the second oldest residence in Yorktown. In the mid-1900s, the Pate House was restored to its former and present appearance—that of an early eighteenth-century English cottage.*

*The Victory figure atop Yorktown's monument seems to guard the town with watchful compassion in this view from the Nelson House. In 1973 Yorktown was named an official state historic landmark and was placed on the National Register of Historic Places. Few towns in the United States suffered so much to earn their niche in American history.*

*Mr. and Mrs. Nick Mathews came to Yorktown in 1944 and began the renowned Nick's Seafood Pavilion on Water Street. The restaurant's famous seafood dishes have brought it a reputation that rivals some of the area's historic attractions. "Mr. Nick" and his wife Mary, who came from the Greek Isles, are noted for their spirited support of Yorktown, and they donated twenty-one acres of land for the Yorktown Victory Center. Their latest acquisition to the collection of statuary standing in their restaurant lobby is a copy of the Winged Victory. The original Victory was erected on the island of Samothrace, possibly to commemorate a naval victory by the Greeks over enemies who came from the sea. The Mathews see their copy as a monument to another naval victory—at Yorktown—where another enemy at another time was defeated.*

*A one-thousand-pound British cannon was recovered from the York River in October 1978, 197 years after it was believed sunk by American and French troops. It is thought to be from the* HMS Charon, *largest warship in Lieutenant General Charles Cornwallis' fleet at the Battle of Yorktown in 1781. Seven ships have been located, six of them thought to be part of Cornwallis' sunken fleet. Divers from the Virginia Research Center for Archaeology spent the summer and well into the fall searching the river bottom off Yorktown and Gloucester Point.*

*The Yorktown Visitor Center adjoining the battlefield was enlarged in 1976. The center provides a film and displays that complement a tour of the historic battlefield. Cannons of the period are located all along the British line of defense, and the pavilion at Surrender Field provides a sweeping view and a recording that explains what happened at the siege and surrender of Yorktown.*

ROCHAMBE

*The historically rich Commonwealth of Virginia had a lot to celebrate during the country's bicentennial in 1976. Virginia's birthday party included opening the Yorktown Victory Center, which probably will remain open after the close of the bicentennial in 1983. The center's offerings include Revolutionary War artifacts, exhibits tracing colonial life and the history of the American Revolution, and the documentary film* The Road to Yorktown. *The center overlooks the York River on almost twenty-two acres of land.*

QUI
HONI

# The Historic Triangle in Color

*These full-sized replicas of the* Susan Constant, Godspeed, *and* Discovery *at Jamestown Festival Park were built in 1957 to celebrate the 350th anniversary of the Jamestown settlement.*

*This figure in colonial Williamsburg guards one of the gates to the Governor's Palace, which was originally completed in 1720.*

*Behind the Brush-Everard house extends a lovely, long garden boasting boxwood actually planted in colonial times. The shrubs, originally bordering the walkways, have grown so large that they now form a centerpiece for rerouted paths.*

*One of the many original restored houses in Williamsburg's historic area that is open to the public is the Brush-Everard House on the east side of the Palace Green. Built in 1777 by John Brush, a gunsmith and first keeper of the Powder Magazine, the frame dwelling later was acquired by Thomas Everard, who was once mayor of the colonial capital. The Brush-Everard House typifies Williamsburg's town houses.*

*Warm colors and a game or puzzle spread on the table seem to suggest that the family which occupied the town house in the late 1700s might return at any moment.*

*The children's room on the second floor fits under the roof across the center hall from the master bedroom. It is attractively furnished in what The Colonial Williamsburg Foundation calls southern colonial style.*

*Fireplaces grace both front rooms on the first floor of the Brush-Everard house, and the furnishings reflect what would have been appropriate for a gentleman of standing in the community.*

*The Nelson House and its elegant garden remain as reminders of one of the Revolutionary War's most overlooked patriots, Thomas Nelson, Jr. Restored by the National Park Service prior to the bicentennial, the Georgian-style mansion still bears scars from the cannon fire that American and French soldiers leveled on Yorktown. Built in 1711, the structure was acquired by Colonial National Historical Park in 1968.*

Approach to Jamestown

Colonial Parkway-Yorktown

Colonial Parkway-near Williamsburg

# Bibliography


Andrews, Matthew Page. *The Soul of a Nation.* New York: Charles Scribner's Sons, 1943.

Barbour, Philip L., ed. *The Jamestown Voyage under The First Charter. 1606-1609.* Vols. I and II. Cambridge: Cambridge Univ. Press, 1969.

Bemiss, Samuel M. *Ancient Adventurers.* Richmond, Virginia: Garrett & Massie, 1964.

Bolitho, Hector. *The Glasshouse, Jamestown, Virginia.* n.p. Jamestown Glasshouse Foundation, 1957.

Bridenbaugh, Carl. *Seat of Empire. The Political Role of Eighteenth Century Williamsburg.* Williamsburg, Va.: Colonial Williamsburg, Inc. 1950.

Bryant, Melville I., Jr. *Yorktown: Reflections on the Past.* n.p. McClure Press, 1974.

Chidsey, Donald Barr. *Victory at Yorktown.* New York: Crown Publishers, Inc., 1962.

Coale, Griffith Baily. *Arrival of the First Permanent English Settlers off Jamestown, Virginia, 13 May 1607.* n.p.: The American Neptune, Inc., 1950.

*Colonial Williamsburg. Official Guidebook and Map.* Williamsburg, Va.: Colonial Williamsburg Foundation, 1972.

Cotter, John L., and J. Paul Hudson. *New Discoveries at Jamestown.* Washington, D.C.: GPO, 1957.

Dabney, Virginius. *Virginia: The New Dominion.* Garden City, N.Y.: Doubleday & Company, 1971.

Davis, J.E. *Jamestown and Her Neighbors. On Virginia's Historic Peninsula.* Richmond, Va.: Garrett & Massie, Inc., Publishers, 1928.

Fee, Robert G.C. "Design and Construction of the Jamestown Ships." Paper presented at the spring meeting, 2-3 June 1958, Society of Naval Architects and Marine Engineers.

Fishwick, Marshall W., and the editors of American Heritage. *Jamestown: First English Colony.* New York: American Heritage Publishing Company, Inc., 1965.

Foster, Mary L. *Colonial Capitals of the Dominion of Virginia.* Lynchburg, Va.: J.P. Bell Company, Inc., 1906.

Friddell, Guy. *We Began at Jamestown.* Richmond, Va.: The Dietz Press, Inc., 1968.

Goodwin, Rutherfoord. *A Brief History of and Guide Book to Jamestown, Williamsburg and Yorktown.* Richmond, Va.: Cottrell & Cooke, Inc., 1930.

Hatch, Charles E., Jr. *"Jamestown, Virginia: The Townsite and Its Story.* Washington, D.C.: National Park Service Historical Handbook Series No. 2, 1949.

______________. *Yorktown and the Siege of 1781.* Washington, D.C.: National Park Service Historical Handbook Series No. 14, 1954. Revised 1957.

Hawthorne, Hildegarde. *Williamsburg Old and New.* n.p.;D. Appleton-Century Company, Inc., 1941.

Hudson, J. Paul. Illustrated by Sidney E. King. *A Pictorial Story of Jamestown, Virginia: The Voyage and Search for a Settlement Site.* Richmond, Va.: Garrett and Massie, Inc., 1975.

Hume, Audrey Noel, et. al. *Five Artifact Studies.* Williamsburg, Va.: Colonial Williamsburg Foundation, 1973.

Johnston, Henry P. *The Yorktown Campaign and the Surrender of Cornwallis 1781.* 1881: rpt. Spartanburg, S.C.: The Reprint Company, 1973.

Kocher, Lawrence A., and Howard Dearstyne. *Colonial Williamsburg. Its Buildings and Gardens.* Williamsburg, Va.: Colonial Williamsburg, Inc., 1949.

Molineux, Will. "House of Giants." *William and Mary Alumni Gazette,* May 1964.

Niles, Blair. Illustrated by Edward Shenton. *The James. From Iron Gate to the Sea.* New York: Farrar & Rinehardt, Inc., 1939.

Osborne, J.A. Illustrated by Elmo Jones. *Williamsburg in Colonial Times.* Intro. W.A.R. Goodwin. 1936; rpt.: Port Washington, N.Y.:Kennikat Press, 1972.

Rose, Grace Norton. Drawings by Jack Manley Rose. *Williamsburg Today & Yesterday.* New York: G.P. Putnam's Sons, 1940.

Rouse, Parke, Jr. *A Pictorial History. Virginia.* New York: Charles Scribner's Sons, 1975.

______________. Official photographs by Thomas L. Williams. *The City That Turned Back Time. Colonial Williamsburg's First Twenty-Five Years.* Williamsburg, Va.: Colonial Williamsburg, Inc., 1952.

______________. *Virginia: The English Heritage in America.* New York: Hastings House Publishers, 1966.

______________. *Planters and Pioneers. Life in Colonial Virginia.* New York: Hastings House Publishers, 1968.

______________. *Cows on the Campus. Williamsburg in Bygone Days.* Richmond, Va.: The Dietz Press, 1973.

Smith, Alan, and B.A. Charles, eds. *Virginia 1584-1607. The First English Settlement in North America.* Boston: Branford Company, n.d.

Swem, E.G., ed. *Jamestown 350th Anniversary Historical Booklets.* Williamsburg, Va.: The Virginia 350th Anniversary Celebration Corporation, 1957.

Thane, Elswyth. *The Virginia Colony.* London: Crowell-Collier Press, Collier-Macmillan Limited, 1969.

Trudell, Clyde F. *Colonial Yorktown.* Illustrated by the author. The Chatham Press, Inc. Old Greenwich, Connecticut: Distributed by the Viking Press, Inc. New York, New York. Copyright 1938, the Dietz Press, Richmond, Virginia. Copyright 1971 by the Eastern National Park and Monument Association.

Walklet, John J., Jr. Photographs by Taylor Biggs Lewis, Jr. *A Window on Williamsburg.* Williamsburg, Va.: Colonial Williamsburg, Inc. 1966.

Williams, Thomas L., photographer. *Williamsburg in Color.* Williamsburg, Va.: Colonial Williamsburg, Inc., 1964.

Wise, Felicity. Illustrations by Penelope Pride. *A Williamsburg Hornbook.* Harrisonburg, Pa.: Stackpole Books, 1973.

# Picture Credits

Page 2: Courtesy of the Daily Press, Inc.

Page 4: Courtesy of Thomas L. Williams

Page 6: Bea Kopp

Page 8: Thom Slater for the Daily Press, Inc.

Page 10: Left-Willard Owens for the Daily Press, Inc.; Right-Courtesy of Thomas G. Pullen, Jr., Scrapbook, College Archives, Swem Library, College of William and Mary

Page 12: Bea Kopp

Page 14: Jamestown-Yorktown Foundation

Page 16: Colonial Williamsburg

Page 17: Herb Barnes for the Daily Press, Inc.

Page 18: Bea Kopp

Page 20: U. S. Air Force

Page 21: Top-The Daily Press, Inc.; Bottom-Herb Barnes for the Daily Press

Page 22: Bea Kopp

Page 23: Top-Herb Barnes for the Daily Press; Bottom-Thom Slater for the Daily Press

Page 24: The Daily Press, Inc.

Page 25: The Daily Press, Inc.

Page 26: Bea Kopp

Page 27: Bea Kopp

Page 28: Left-Joe Fudge for the Daily Press, Inc.; Right-Jamestown-Yorktown Foundation.

Page 29: Top-Jamestown-Yorktown Foundation; Bottom-Colonial National Historical Park Photograph Collection

Page 30: Joe Fudge for the Daily Press, Inc.

Page 31: Jamestown-Yorktown Foundation

Page 32: Top-Jamestown-Yorktown Foundation; Bottom-Jamestown-Yorktown Foundation

Page 33: Colonial National Historical Park Photograph Collection

Page 34: Top-Jamestown-Yorktown Foundation; Bottom-Virginia State Library

Page 35: Harper's Weekly

Page 36: Top-The Daily Press, Inc.; Bottom-The Daily Press, Inc.

Page 37: Top-Bea Kopp; Bottom-Bea Kopp

Page 38: "The Peninsula of Virginia" by the late Harry R. Houston

Page 39: Bea Kopp

Page 40: Left-Willard Owens for the Daily Press, Inc.; Right-Courtesy of Thomas G. Pullen, Jr., Scrapbook, College Archives, Swem Library, College of William and Mary

Page 41: Top-Bea Kopp; Bottom-Bea Kopp

Page 42: Top-Bea Kopp; Bottom-Bea Kopp

Page 43: Willard Owens for the Daily Press, Inc.

Page 44: Top-Thom Slater for the Daily Press, Inc.; Bottom-Herb Barnes for the Daily Press, Inc.

Page 45: Bea Kopp

Page 46 and 47: The Daily Press, Inc.

Page 48: Bea Kopp

Page 50: Colonial Williamsburg

Page 51: Jamestown-Yorktown Foundation

Page 52: The College of William and Mary in Virginia

Page 53: The Daily Press, Inc.

Page 54: Top-Bea Kopp; Bottom-Bea Kopp

Page 55: Top-Bea Kopp; Bottom-Bea Kopp

Page 56: Top-Courtesy of Thomas G. Pullen, Jr., Scrapbook, College Archives, Swem Library, College of William and Mary; Bottom-Courtesy of Thomas L. Williams

Page 57: Top-Bea Kopp; Bottom-Courtesy of Dr. Janet Kimbrough

Page 58: Top-Courtesy of Dr. Janet Kimbrough; Bottom-Courtesy of Thomas L. Williams

Page 59: Top-Bea Kopp; Bottom-Courtesy of Dr. Janet Kimbrough

Page 60: Thom Slater for the Daily Press, Inc.

Page 61: Colonial Williamsburg

Page 62: Top-Bea Kopp; Bottom-Bea Kopp

Page 63: Bea Kopp

Page 64: Top-Bea Kopp; Bottom-Bea Kopp

Page 65: Top-Bea Kopp; Bottom-Courtesy of Dr. Janet Kimbrough

Page 66: Top Left and Top Right-Courtesy of Thomas L. Williams; Bottom-Colonial Williamsburg

Page 67: Colonial Williamsburg

Page 68: Top-Bea Kopp; Bottom-Colonial Williamsburg

Page 69: Bea Kopp

Page 70: Top-Bea Kopp; Bottom-Colonial Williamsburg

Page 71: Colonial Williamsburg

Page 72: Top-Colonial Williamsburg; Bottom-Colonial Williamsburg

Page 73: Bea Kopp

Page 74: Bea Kopp

Page 75: Bea Kopp

Page 76: Left-Jamestown-Yorktown Foundation; Right-Colonial Williamsburg

Page 77: Colonial Williamsburg

Page 78: Top-Bea Kopp; Bottom-Bea Kopp

Page 79: Bea Kopp

Page 80: Colonial Williamsburg

Page 81: Bea Kopp

Page 82: Top-Bea Kopp; Bottom-Thom Slater for the Daily Press, Inc.

Page 83: Top-Bea Kopp; Middle-Bea Kopp; Bottom-Bea Kopp

Page 84: Top-Bea Kopp; Bottom-Colonial Williamsburg

Page 85: Bea Kopp

Page 86: Bea Kopp

Page 87: Top-Courtesy of Thomas L. Williams; Bottom-Courtesy of Dr. Janet Kimbrough

Page 88: Thom Slater for the Daily Press, Inc.

Page 89: Top-The College of William and Mary in Virginia; Bottom-Courtesy of Dr. Janet Kimbrough

Page 90: Top-Property of the Anne Galt Black Collection; Bottom-Bea Kopp

Page 91: Top-Eastern State Hospital; Bottom-Bea Kopp

Page 92: Top and Bottom-Courtesy of Thomas G. Pullen, Jr., Scrapbook, College Archives, Swem Library, College of William and Mary

Page 93: Top and Bottom-Courtesy of Dr. Janet Kimbrough

Page 94: Top-Colonial Williamsburg; Bottom-Courtesy of Thomas G. Pullen, Jr., Scrapbook, College Archives, Swem Library, College of William and Mary

Page 95: Top and Bottom-Colonial Williamsburg

Page 96: Top-Courtesy of Thomas L. Williams; Bottom-Courtesy of Dr. Janet Kimbrough

Page 97: Top-Colonial Williamsburg; Bottom-Courtesy of Thomas L. Williams

Page 98: Top and Bottom-Colonial Williamsburg

Page 99: Bea Kopp

Page 100: Top-Courtesy of Thomas L. Williams; Bottom Left-Courtesy of Thomas L. Williams; Bottom Right-Courtesy of Thomas G. Pullen, Jr., Scrapbook, College Archives, Swem Library, College of William and Mary

Page 101: Courtesy of Dr. Janet Kimbrough

Page 102: Top and Bottom-Courtesy of Thomas L. Williams

Page 103: Top and Bottom-Courtesy of Dr. Janet Kimbrough

Page 104: Top Left-Courtesy of Mrs. Henry M. Stryker; Top Right-Courtesy of Carleton Casey; Bottom-The College of William and Mary in Virginia

Page 105: Top-Courtesy of Dr. Janet Kimbrough; Bottom-The College of William and Mary in Virginia

Page 106: Top-Courtesy of Thomas G. Pullen, Jr., Scrapbook, College Archives, Swem Library, College of William and Mary Bottom-Courtesy of Dr. Janet Kimbrough

Page 107: Top-Courtesy of Dr. Janet Kimbrough; Bottom-Colonial Williamsburg

Page 108: Top-Colonial Williamsburg; Bottom-Colonial Williamsburg

Page 109: Top-Colonial Williamsburg; Bottom-Colonial Williamsburg

Page 110: Top-Colonial Williamsburg; Bottom-Colonial Williamsburg

Page 111: Top-The College of William and Mary in Virginia; Bottom-The College of William and Mary in Virginia

Page 112: Left and Right-Courtesy of Dr. Janet Kimbrough

Page 113: Left-The College of William and Mary in Virginia; Right-The College of William and Mary in Virginia

Page 114: Top Left-Courtesy of Mrs. Henry M. Stryker; Top Right-Courtesy of Dr. Janet Kimbrough; Bottom Left-Bea Kopp

Page 115: Joe Fudge for the Daily Press, Inc.

Page 116: Top-Bea Kopp; Bottom-Henry M. Stryker

Page 117: Left-Thom Slater for the Daily Press, Inc.; Right-The College of William and Mary in Virginia

Page 118: Top Left-Bea Kopp; Top Right-Thom Slater for the Daily Press, Inc.; Bottom-Bea Kopp

Page 119: Top-Bea Kopp; Center-Bea Kopp; Bottom-Thom Slater for the Daily Press, Inc.

Page 120: Top Left-Thom Slater for the Daily Press, Inc.; Bottom Left-Thom Slater for the Daily Press, Inc.

Page 121: Top Left and Right-Courtesy of Carleton Casey

Page 120-121: Bottom-The Daily Press, Inc.

Page 122: Top-Bea Kopp; Bottom Left-Bea Kopp

Page 123: Top Right-Colonial Williamsburg; Bottom-Bea Kopp

Page 124: Top Left-The Common Glory-Swem Library; Bottom-The Common Glory-Swem Library

Page 125: Top-The Common Glory-Swem Library; Bottom-The Common Glory-Swem Library

Page 126: Top-Joe Fudge for the Daily Press, Inc.; Bottom- Joe Fudge for the Daily Press, Inc.

Page 127: Top-Joe Fudge for the Daily Press, Inc.; Bottom-Thom Slater for the Daily Press, Inc.

Page 128: Top Left-Bea Kopp; Top Right-Thom Slater for the Daily Press, Inc.; Bottom-Thom Slater for the Daily Press, Inc.

Page 129: Top-Jim Livengood; Bottom: Jim Livengood

Page 130: Bea Kopp

Page 132: Top-Joe Fudge for the Daily Press, Inc.; Bottom Left-Bea Kopp

Page 133: Top-Bea Kopp; Center-Bea Kopp; Bottom-Bea Kopp

Page 134: Top-The Mariners Museum, Newport News, Virginia; Bottom-Jamestown-Yorktown Foundation

Page 135: Top- Colonial National Historical Park Photograph Collection; Bottom Right-Family Magazine

Page 136: Top- Colonial National Historical Park Photograph Collection; Bottom- Colonial National Historical Park Photograph Collection

Page 137: Top Left- Colonial National Historical Park Photograph Collection; Top Right- Colonial National Historical Park Photograph Collection; Bottom Right-Colonial Williamsburg

Page 138: Bottom-The Daily Press, Inc.

Page 139: Top Right-Herb Barnes for the Daily Press, Inc.

Pages 138 and 139: Top-The Daily Press, Inc.

Page 140: Top-The Daily Press, Inc.; Bottom-Collection of the Chrysler Museum at Norfolk, Gift of the Norfolk Newspapers' Art Trust Fund

Page 141: Top-Sebastian Bauman Map

Page 142: Top-Bea Kopp; Bottom-Bea Kopp

Page 143: Bea Kopp

Page 144: Top-Virginia State Library;

Page 145: Bea Kopp; Inset- Colonial National Historical Park Photograph Collection

Page 146: Left-Joe Fudge for the Daily Press, Inc.; Right-Bea Kopp

Page 147: Colonial National Historical Park Photograph Collection

Pages 148 and 149: Mrs. Dorothy R. Bottom

Page 150: Bea Kopp

Page 151: The Daily Press, Inc.

Page 152: Top-Bea Kopp; Bottom-Bea Kopp

Page 153: Bea Kopp

Page 154: Top- Colonial National Historical Park Photograph Collection; Bottom- Colonial National Historical Park Photograph Collection

Page 155: Top- Colonial National Historical Park Photograph Collection; Bottom- Colonial National Historical Park Photograph Collection

Page 156: The Peninsula of Virginia by the late Harry R. Houston

Page 157: The Peninsula of Virginia by the late Harry R. Houston

Page 158: Top-Harper's Weekly; Bottom-The Daily Press, Inc.

Page 159: Top Left-Joe Fudge for the Daily Press, Inc.; Right-Bea Kopp

Page 160: Top-The Daily Press, Inc.; Bottom- Colonial National Historical Park Photograph Collection

Page 161: The Daily Press, Inc.

Page 162: Top-Bea Kopp; Bottom-Bea Kopp

Page 163: Bea Kopp

Page 164: Courtesy of Dr. Janet Kimbrough

Page 165: Top and Bottom-Courtesy of Dr. Janet Kimbrough

Page 166: Top-Colonial National Historical Park Photograph Collection; Bottom; Colonial National Historical Park Photograph Collection

Page 167: Top-U. S. Army; Bottom: The Daily Press, Inc.

Page 168: Top-The Daily Press, Inc.; Bottom; Bea Kopp

Page 169: Top-Thom Slater for the Daily Press, Inc.; Bottom-The Daily Press, Inc.

Page 170: Bottom-Bea Kopp

Page 171: Right-Courtesy of Dr. Janet Kimbrough

Pages 170 and 171: Top-Bea Kopp

Page 172: Top-Bea Kopp; Bottom-Bea Kopp

Page 173: Bea Kopp

Page 174: Bea Kopp

Page 175: Bea Kopp

Page 176: Willard Owens for the Daily Press, Inc.

Page 177: Willard Owens for the Daily Press, Inc.

Page 178: Top-Bea Kopp; Botom-Bea Kopp

Page 179: Top-Bea Kopp; Bottom-Bea Kopp

Pages 180 and 181: Bea Kopp

Color Section photographs courtesy of Bea Kopp